Farrel & Sherman Herring

Fighting Fire for twenty-six Years

Farrel & Sherman Herring

Fighting Fire for twenty-six Years

ISBN/EAN: 9783337149031

Printed in Europe, USA, Canada, Australia, Japan

Cover: Foto ©ninafisch / pixelio.de

More available books at **www.hansebooks.com**

FIGHTING FIRE

FOR

TWENTY-SIX YEARS,

BEING

THE ACTUAL EXPERIENCE OF

HERRING'S CELEBRATED SAFES,

IN MORE THAN

FIVE HUNDRED ACCIDENTAL TRIALS,

With the Testimonials of their Owners.

---•·•---

PUBLISHED BY
HERRING, FARREL & SHERMAN, 251 BROADWAY, NEW YORK.
FARREL, HERRING & CO., No. 629 CHESTNUT STREET, PHILADELPHIA.
HERRING, FARREL & SHERMAN, 72 CAMP ST., NEW ORLEANS.
HERRING & CO., No. 10 STATE STREET, CHICAGO.

CONTENTS.

	PAGE
FIRES IN MAINE...................................	9
" MASSACHUSETTS...........................	11
" CONNECTICUT..............................	12
" RHODE ISLAND.............................	14
" NEW YORK..................................	36
" NEW YORK CITY............................	15
" NEW JERSEY................................	70
" PENNSYLVANIA.............................	62
" PHILADELPHIA..............................	58
" DISTRICT COLUMBIA.......................	73
" RICHMOND..................................	73
" VIRGINIA....................................	79
" NORTH CAROLINA..........................	82
" SOUTH CAROLINA..........................	83
" GEORGIA....................................	86
" ALABAMA...................................	92
" FLORIDA....................................	90
" MISSISSIPPI.................................	94
" LOUISIANA..................................	95
" TEXAS.......................................	98
" ARKANSAS..................................	99
" TENNESSEE.................................	103
" MISSOURI...................................	100
" OHIO..	104
" INDIANA....................................	112
" ILLINOIS....................................	109
" WISCONSIN.................................	113
" MICHIGAN..................................	106
" IOWA..	116
" MINNESOTA.................................	117
" CALIFORNIA................................	119
" KANSAS.....................................	118
" COLORADO.................................	119
" CANADA....................................	122
" ISTHMUS OF PANAMA.......................	125
" WEST INDIES...............................	125
" JAPAN......................................	124
GREAT BANK ROBBERY.............................	127

AWARDED

HERRING'S PATENT FIRE-PROOF SAFES.

LONDON.
1851.

ALSO AT THE

CRYSTAL PALACE.

NEW YORK.
1853.

In addition to the foregoing,

GOLD AND SILVER MEDALS AND DIPLOMAS

Have been awarded the Subscribers for their

SAFES AND LOCKS,

By the following Societies and Institutions, viz:

AMERICAN INSTITUTE, New York. FRANKLIN INSTITUTE, Philadelphia.
METROPOLITAN MECHANICS' INSTITUTE, VIRGINIA STATE FAIR, Richmond, Va.
Washington, D. C. MISSOURI STATE FAIR, St. Louis, Mo.
PENNSYLVANIA STATE FAIR, and many others.

PREFACE.

The atmosphere heated to a certain point, being deprived of its oxygen, combustion is the consequence. To produce a barrier, if not an effectual limit, to combustion in certain cases has been our constant study for more than a quarter of a century. No human agency can control or prevent the origin of conflagration; and it has been our aim, so far as our experience and ability give us the power, to say to the fiery dragon: "Thus far shalt thou go and no farther."

From the beginning of time water has been the favorite antidote for fire, and it has been the unfailing resort to prevent and check the march of the devouring element. Yet, it is known that in the burning of certain compounds the application of water is but adding fuel to the flames. Water, notwithstanding its many virtues, is not always reliable either as an extinguisher or a preventive of fire.

It is upon the "water theory," however, that until a very recent period, all portable fire-proof safes have been built. It will surprise some to learn that the first safes (?) or chests manufactured in this country were lined or filled with wood—a singular protection, many of our readers will observe, but no less a fact; and there are those who well remember the old-fashioned "knob-chests," as they were called, which were simply wooden boxes covered first with thin sheet iron, then banded and strapped, and the whole nailed fast with large nails, having prominent knobs or cast-iron heads to imitate or represent the strong rivets of a boiler.

These "formidable"-looking chests will be recollected as the strong-box or safe of the merchants' counting room in the olden time. They, indeed, have almost passed away; yet, singular enough, the theory upon which these wooden "fire-proofs" were first made has been the theory upon which iron safe manufacturers have from that time to this, been constantly building.

Although it may seem strange that wood was ever used as a fire-proof protector in safes, yet it must be borne in mind that the original plan was to prepare the wood for this purpose before applying it to the safe. It is well known that though wood is highly combustible, it is really a poor *conductor* of heat, and when protected from the atmosphere so as to prevent ignition it will transmit heat very slowly. Take, for example, a small piece of wood; apply to one side of it all the heat you choose; so long as the wood does not ignite, of course you cannot burn paper *through it.* Iron or metals are directly opposite in their nature. They resist combustion to a far greater extent, but more readily convey or conduct the heat through them.

The original method of preparing wood as a lining or fire-proof filling for safes was to saturate or soak it with salt water or brine, and as the wood is a ready absorbent, having a great affinity for water, it retained this saturation for some time; consequently, when exposed to the fire, the wood gave out its moisture, the fibre charred in place of igniting, and combustion proceeded slowly. Alas for the safe-makers of those days, however; their work became their ruin! It was found in the course of time that saturation produced decay, and in the lapse of a few years the fire-proof lining began to perish, and the wood became a mass of dry rot, liable almost to take fire by itself from spontaneous combustion. Many of these old chests are known to have taken fire when in this decomposed state through no agency but the near proximity of the counting-room stove.

The next period in safe-making and the date of our advent in the business is now known as the plaster of Paris or cement age—the water, considered as a necessity to retard the action of the fire, being this time retained by plaster or hydraulic cements, which, becoming hard and rock-like, were then supposed to be unchangeable.

The story of the origin of this plan of "fire-proofing" is a little romantic. It is said that an industrious mechanic was one day engaged in making moulds or casts with plaster of Paris. Having finished his labors he was preparing to wash up, and for this purpose he attempted to heat some water in a kettle in which he had mixed his calcined plaster. After stirring his fire impatiently on several occasions he was surprised to find that the water did not warm up with its accustomed rapidity, and a further inspection showed the bottom of the kettle retained the debris of his plaster-mixings. Upon their removal the difficulty was obviated. This gave him the idea of its non-conducting powers and suggested it as a lining for fire-proof repositories. About the same time an old and well-known type-founder of this city, now deceased, but whose sons are still prominent as his successors, had noticed and remarked the non-conducting power of plaster of Paris when mixed with water, as he was constantly using it in his business, and had actually constructed or lined a safe with this fire-proof composition as a protection for valuables in his possession.[*]

The priority of invention is still claimed by both parties. But certain it is that this was the beginning of the plaster of Paris filling for fire-proof safes, so long and so tenaciously clung to.

The first attempts in this case, like most first attempts, proved failures. The calcined plaster was of no use as a fire-proof cement unless mixed with water. Still the misfortune remained that the damp compound would mould

---

[*] This safe, the first one ever filled with plaster of Paris, and made nearly forty years ago, is now in our store.

and destroy books and papers in the safe if it was kept closed, and could not protect them from fire if left open. It was about this time that the senior member of our firm came to the rescue, and after many experiments produced plaster of Paris lined safes that were comparatively dry for the counting-room, and made the first truly popular safes in use on this continent.

Time, however, the great teacher, demonstrated that plaster of Paris *without* water, as a protection from fire, is not much better than so much sand, and the mixture of water necessary to secure its non-conducting qualities would gradually evaporate or dry out, in which operation it oxydized the iron box in which it was confined. Thus, besides losing some of its fire-proof qualities with age, it also rusted, or "rotted out," the iron of the safe in time, thereby always carrying within itself the seeds of its own destruction.

The Plaster of Paris Safe, or "Wilder Patent of 1843," for which we made all the good reputation it ever had, was simply plaster of Paris mixed with water, the fire-proof property consisting in the ability of the plaster to absorb and retain a large amount of water. While new and its effects upon the iron not suspected, we used it as the best thing known *at that time*.

As, however, experience developed its defects, and it became apparent that the water would gradually evaporate, causing the contents of the safe to mould and mildew and the iron of the outside to rust, we determined to benefit the public and ourselves by the experience we had gained and to bring out all the ingenuity available by offering large rewards for the production of a better and more enduring fire-proof filling than plaster of Paris had proved to be.

Invention was again busy. "Croton Water Safes" were talked of; these to be made stationary, and the water to be let on by the burning of a string or the melting of a soft cement faucet on the approach of heat. Alum and clay were recommended, still adhering to the old water theory to produce steam in case of fire. But these were only partial remedies, and experience has proved that they were not reliable in accidental fires. Premiums were offered for dry fire-proof fillings, and the result has been a steady and constant improvement in fire-proof protectors where properly made; and demonstrated that too much water is as dangerous to the safe as too little; as water itself, or materials containing a large amount of that element, are known to evaporate or lose their qualities at a low temperature. Water itself boils at 212 degrees and is soon dissipated at a higher heat. It is not so much the quantity of moisture that is required to keep out heat in a safe as the *quality*. It is not the material which will hold the most water that is best for fire-proof filling, but one that will hold its peculiar moisture *the longest* when operated against by accidental fire.

Carefully pursuing this plan in place of the old water theory, the Herring Safe has not only maintained its position in the front rank, but quite recent fires have shown it to be very far in advance of all others.

It is well known that the production of certain atmospheres are antagonistic to heat, and in the presence of a certain air or gas no flame can live. The production of the Herring's Patent Composition demonstrated that, though it did not secrete so much moisture, yet it was more slowly evaporated or driven out by fire than any other compound heretofore known; and the more recent improvements which we have secured by patents within the past two years have proved that a fire-proof filling for safes is produced that is perfectly dry and unchangeable until the fire attacks it, which will not dampen or mould books and papers, will not corrode or rust the iron of the safe, and does not dry out or lose any of its fire-proof qualities from evaporation in a warm room. In place of boiling at 212° – the boiling point of water – its fumes are noticeable at the red heat of iron (1,000°); and our fire-proof lining being a double sulphate, it produces an atmosphere in which, so long as it lasts, no flame can exist.

The patents of S. C. Herring of May 18, 1852, improved and renewed May 18, 1866, and of John Farrel, February 7, 1865, produce the most perfect and complete

DRY SAFE, THAT IS ALSO RELIABLE AGAINST FIRE,

ever offered to the public.

Another great advantage with our new patent filling is—that while it is put in as a powder, dry as flour, when subjected to a hot fire it fuses or combines into a compact mass; does not decrepitate or lose its bulk, or leave large holes and vacancies in the fire-proof filling, as other compositions do. It becomes solid and firm, giving also additional strength to the body of the safe when exposed amid falling ruins.

With the increased growth of our cities and towns and constantly increasing size of our mercantile warehouses, we require more than ever the best and strongest safes. Iron columns, iron beams, and iron girders are fast displacing wooden ones in our modern buildings, and in the conflagration these falling masses of iron need more than common safes to ward their heavy blows.

Having these important requirements in view, we have also made many improvements in the strength and mechanism of our work. Besides improved beauty of finish, the entire body of the safe is made all of *wrought*-iron and much heavier than heretofore. Our frames are manufactured from the best refined wrought-iron and are welded (not matched) together. Our corners are *solid*, of the best wrought angle-iron, in place of matched bars or cast iron corners, so common with other safes. We have also just completed an entire new set of patterns, which will give increased thickness of fire-proof filling, so that with improved fire and rust proof filling, improved strength and weight of metal, and improved patterns, it shall be our aim, as it ever has been, to give to the public " the best safe the world ever saw," and furnish it at a fair price, consistent with good work. How well we have succeeded so far the public are the judges; and that we shall hereafter "surpass ourselves" is the pledge we make to our many liberal patrons.

NEW YORK, January 1, 1867.

AN INTERESTING HISTORY.

Twenty-six years ago the senior member of our firm commenced his career in the safe business. Previous to that date, with the exception of a few spasmodic efforts, most all safe manufacturers had confined their operations to safes or chests lined with wood, made after the pattern of a few that were first imported from France.

The great trial of safes at Coffee-house Slip, foot of Wall street, New York, in 1840, in which all the leading fire-proof chests then made were destroyed, while the newly introduced Salamander bore off the palm of victory, was witnessed by Mr. Herring, and first induced him to engage in reanimating its fortunes. Previous to his embarking in the enterprise the history of the Salamander had been one of misfortune, owing to the want of means and ability of those having it in charge, and the natural slowness of the public to encourage new productions. The existence of the new safe had been a fitful and uncertain one. The want of experience in the manufacture and the imperfect manner in which they had been made had discouraged and bankrupted those who had at first attempted it, and its reputation had reached a very low point when Herring's name first became associated with the enterprise.

Energy and perseverance, however, are most certain to bring their reward, particularly where merit is really the basis of the structure. Beginning with the determination that a good safe was attainable, and that the public should always receive their money's worth, the popularity of the Herring's safe demonstrates how well that resolution had been adhered to, and its consequent reward. Twenty-six years ago the first stock of safes was contained in a little room not more than 20 by 40 feet, and though prices then only ranged from $40 to $250, the sales of safes were very slow. Shortly afterward, for economy's sake, the building first employed as a sales-room was turned into a manufactory. The basement was the blacksmith's shop, or forging-room, and filling-room. The first floor was the sales and paint-room. The two upper stories were occupied by the iron-workers, who cut the iron, framed the safes, and the one solitary locksmith, who could furnish all the locks as fast as the safes were ready for them. Here everything was under the eye of the proprietor, and all worked for the production of a good article. The many imperfections of the first manufacture were gradually overcome, and the public began slowly to appreciate the enterprise.

The great fires of 1845 gave the first impetus to what has since become a great business, when old-fashioned fire-proof securities proved false to their professions, and even solid vaults of stone and brick yielded to the fiery adversary; the Herring Salamander won its first laurels, and was accepted by the community as the "coming safe," and stepped into the position it has since so well retained as "the best security from fire now known."

The burning of the Tribune buildings and the great fire in this city (which destroyed 400 buildings), and in other cities during that memorable year, when the Herring's safe so well earned its claims to public trust and confidence, created an era in this branch of domestic manufacture. Greater facilities and larger buildings were required for the work; steam power and machinery were brought into requisition, and the clink of the hammer and the song of the workman evinced that a new field of enterprise had been opened which was to help, in its place, to spread the fame of American ingenuity and add another permanent means to the prosperity of the commonwealth. Twenty-six years ago, and two or three safes a week were the limit of production; since then more than thirty thousand of Herring's Safes have gone on their way, messengers of hope and trust to the civilized community, and earning a good name for themselves, and a reputation for their country. The first safes were not, of course, perfections, and countless have been the improvements which experience has suggested and which are continually in progress. The old Salamander gave way to the Champion; Wet-filled safes have been superseded by the dry-filled; boiler-iron has taken the place of sheet-iron in the manufacture, and the days of mouldy safes, rusty safes and dried-out safes are now being succeeded by those which are damp-proof, rust-proof, and whose fire-proof elements or compositions are the results of nearly thirty years of study and experience, and will not dry out or lose their fire-proof qualities by age.

Twenty-six years ago, and a dozen hands, all told, comprised the pay-roll of Herring's Safe manufactory. Now more than three hundred hands are constantly employed in the work on Herring's Safes. Then a five-hundred-dollar safe was a large sale; but now a single safe, or vault, as it is called, is made at a cost of nearly twenty thousand dollars.

One of the Safes from the Great Fire at Portland, Me.

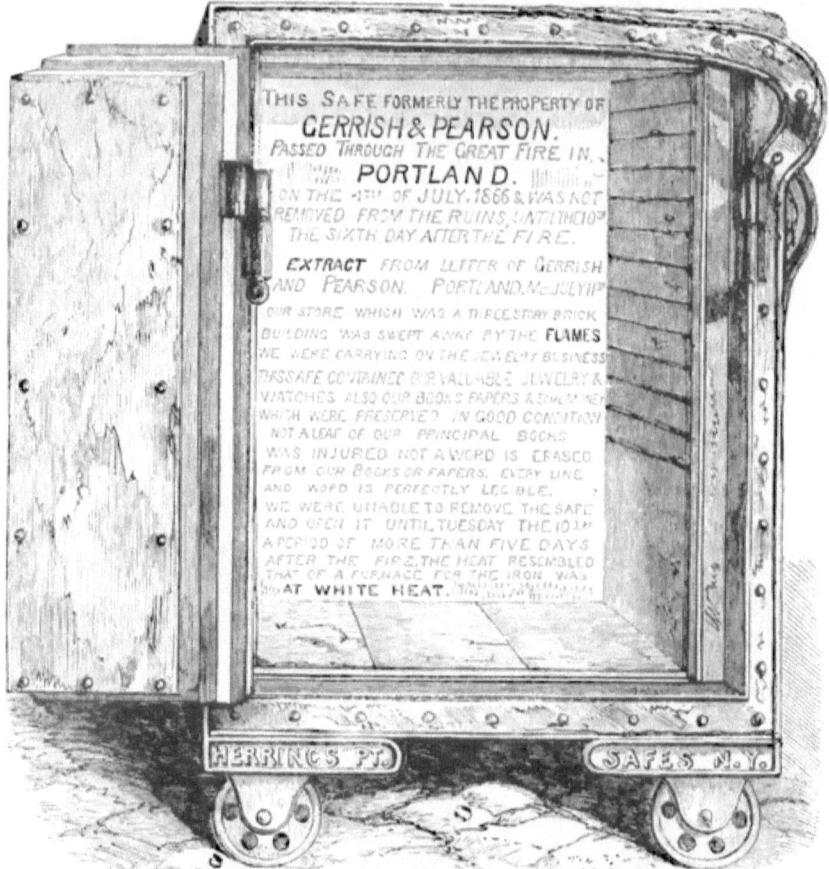

HERRING'S SAFES IN THE LATE PORTLAND CONFLAGRATION.

There is a moral to be drawn from one of the incidents of the late disastrous fire in Portland, that should be carefully considered by those who would avoid a danger that is all the more insidious because we are apt to imagine ourselves secure from it. We refer to the test that has been applied to the Safes of different manufacturers that were exposed to the terrible ordeal of fire there. The word SAFE, which is applied to the iron chests or boxes that are manufactured by all makers, is only applicable, in reality, to such as have stood the test, and our columns show that the Herring Safe fairly sustains the reputation it long ago acquired, of being one of the most perfect fire-proofs yet made. After seeing the reports of the great losses of valuables contained in other safes, we were led to inquire why people should be so blind to their own interests as to trust their treasures in such insecure depositories, when others, that had been proved and tried in hundreds of fires, could be had, and we were informed that in this, as in many other matters, people forget the motto, "The best is the cheapest," and that one cause of the greatest loss in this instance was, that the Portland merchants had purchased safes manufactured in the East that were cheaper than Herring could afford to sell his for. We should as soon trust our funds to a street broker, who might offer a larger interest, than the more cautious and well-known neighboring banker, as put our valuables in an iron box that will not stand the test of fire; and having experienced the satisfaction of owning one of Herring's safes, we the more cheerfully recommend them to our friends.—*Scottish American Journal.*

HERRING'S PATENT
CHAMPION FIRE-PROOF SAFES.

The following collection of voluntary tributes to the excellency and trustworthiness of "HERRING'S SAFES" are presented to the commercial community, as comprising an amount of appreciative and flattering testimony from the most authenticated and highly respectable sources never before equaled in this or any other country.

In the language of the *New York Tribune*, when speaking of the performances of *their own* Herring Safe, which had been buried in the burning ruins of the Tribune Buildings for thirty-six hours, we will say : " How much better another may do, we know not ; but that this did its work nobly, we most heartily testify."

MAINE.

THE GREAT FIRE AT PORTLAND, JULY 4, 1866.

This great conflagration, which destroyed nearly one-half the city, burned over a space of two hundred acres, and destroyed no less than fifteen hundred buildings. The loss was estimated at $12,000,000 ; and unfortunately many lost their books of account, valuable papers, and their all, by trusting to miscalled " Fire-proof " Safes. Indeed, the telegraph, in its hurry to furnish " news," reported all over the land, on the *second day* after the fire, that " most iron safes had proved worthless." This may have been true so far as it went, but the HERRING'S SAFES were still lying under that burning pile, and remained there from three to twenty days, yet saved all their contents in the best of order. *Not one* of Herring's safes failed—let the public bear this in mind ; for these safes were exposed in the hottest of that fire, and side by side with other so-called " Fire-proofs," which proved but mere ovens for valuables they were expected to preserve.

Letter from Gerrish & Pearson.

PORTLAND, July 11, 1866.

Messrs. Herring, Farrel & Sherman, 251 Broadway, New York :

GENTLEMEN—The Fourth of July, with its usual festivities and pleasures, came to a sad termination on the afternoon of that day by the breaking out of the largest fire that ever took place in this country, destroying half of the business portion of the city, with numerous dwellings. Our store, which was in a three-story brick building, was completely swept away by the devouring flames. We were carrying on the jewelry business. We had one of your large-size Champion Safes in use, which contained our valuable jewelry and watches, also our books, papers, and some money, which were preserved in good condition. The covers of the books and some of the watches and jewelry are discolored by the steam from the fire-proof composition; not a leaf of our principal books is injured, not a word is erased from our books or papers, *every line and word perfectly legible;* our jewelry and watches can be cleaned. We were unable to remove this safe and open it until Tuesday, the 10th—a period of more than *five days after the fire.* The heat around it was of the most intense character, as its exterior distinctly shows, the iron being badly warped and sprung. The brass knobs and ornamental plates on the doors were entirely *melted off.* The heat closely resembled that of a furnace, for the iron was at *a white heat.* We would add, that a safe which will preserve its contents in such a fire proves its superiority and is thoroughly fire-proof.

GERRISH & PEARSON.

Letter from N. P. Richardson & Co.

PORTLAND, July 13, 1866.

Messrs. Herring, Farrel & Sherman, 251 Broadway, New York:

GENTLEMEN—The large fire which occurred July 4, entirely destroyed our extensive stove manufactory; also our office, which was in a separate wooden building, two stories in height. The safe, one of your Herring's Patent Champion, was in the *second story;* it fell to the ground. We got it out during the fire by means of chains. *It was red-hot.* We had it cut open on Saturday. The books and papers contained in it were all preserved.

Yours, truly,
N. P. RICHARDSON & CO.

Letter from Edward Shaw, Esq.

PORTLAND, July 10, 1866.

Messrs. Herring, Farrel & Sherman, 251 Broadway, New York:

GENTLEMEN—This once beautiful city has been the scene of the most terrible conflagration ever known in the history of fires on this continent. Fifteen hundred buildings were destroyed, covering an area of more than two hundred acres, reaching a mile and one-half in length, by an average of half a mile in width. The building in which we had the office of the Portland Mutual Fire Insurance Company was entirely consumed. We had a large number of books and papers; these, with other valuables, were all locked up in one of your large-size fire-proof safes. We dug it out of the ruins on Saturday, where it remained three days and a half. After cutting it open, to our great surprise and gratification the contents were preserved in excellent condition; the covers of the books were drawn by the steam of the fire-proof composition. Every line and word in our books and papers are perfectly legible; not a leaf of our books or a paper shows the mark of fire. When we take into consideration the magnitude of this fire, the terrific heat to which your safe was subjected—no water having been thrown on the ruins or on the fire—proves your safe to be perfectly fire-proof. The ordeal through which safes have passed in this severe test—many having been completely burned up—warrant us in saying that too much praise cannot be bestowed on "the Herring," as *every one of your make preserved its contents.*

Respectfully yours,
EDWARD SHAW,
Treas. of P. M. F. Ins. Co.

Letter from J. B. Brown & Sons.

PORTLAND, July 16, 1866.

Messrs. Herring, Farrel & Sherman, 251 Broadway, New York:

GENTLEMEN—The devastating fire which took place in our city on the afternoon of July 4, unparalleled in extent and number of buildings destroyed by any fire that ever took place in this country, entirely consumed our large sugar-house and office. We were using one of your large-size folding-door safes. It was in the

Plate No. 1.

SIZE No. 2.

12 in. high,
8 in. wide, } Inside.
9 in. deep,

SIZE No. 3.

11 in. high,
10 in. wide, } Inside.
10 in. deep,

SIZE No. 4.

16 in. high,
12 in. wide, } Inside.
12 in. deep,

SIZE No. 5.

20 in. high,
15 in. wide, } Inside.
13 in. deep,

third story of our office; when the floor gave way it fell into the cellar on a heap of burning sugar, where it remained until Thursday, when we removed it and had it cut open; it contained our general books, valuable papers, insurance policies, a record of our government bonds, two thousand dollars in bank bills, and some currency. All of them were preserved in excellent order *and a mark of fire on them!* Every line is perfectly legible. The covers of the books were drawn by the steam from the fire-proof filling; they can be rebound; the leaves are perfect. This safe was subjected to a very severe test. We are very much pleased with the result. It has proved itself perfectly fire-proof, and too much praise cannot be awarded to a safe which stood the test so well.

Respectfully yours,   J. B. BROWN & SONS.

Letter from F. O. J. Smith.

(THIS SAFE WAS NOT TAKEN OUT UNTIL TWENTY DAYS AFTER THE FIRE.)

PORTLAND, August 15, 1866.

Messrs. Herring, Farrel & Sherman, 251 Broadway, New York:

GENTLEMEN — A reliable iron safe that will withstand the heat of a conflagration so intense and irresistible as was that which occurred in this city on the 4th and 5th ultimo is more than the equivalent of a solvent and prompt insurance company to a business man. And it affords me pleasure to testify that a safe which I had of your manufacture in the "International House" when destroyed by that terrible fire, proved itself absolutely indestructible, with all its interior contents unharmed, amid the total reduction to ashes of every thing around and near it. The "International" was a building mainly of wood, one hundred and ten feet long by fifty wide, four stories high, with a double roof, one flat and one sharp above, and had at least *one hundred and twenty thousand* feet of lumber in its structure, every foot of which was burnt above and around this safe. I had another safe, made by some unknown person, in the story above and not far from directly over that manufactured by you, and which was buried in the same ruins, within a few feet of yours, the contents of which — papers, books, and wood-work — were reduced to the finest ashes, proving itself *utterly worthless*. As these safes were near the end of the building to which the high wind rushed the entire flame and heat of the burning mass, no spot in the whole city could have had a more intense fire upon it than the one they occupied. They were both left in the heated débris for a fortnight or more after the fire, and on being exhumed were found in the different conditions stated; yours proving itself an absolutely perfect protection to everything intrusted to it, and the other a mere coffin to the dead ashes to which its contents had been reduced. I need not say more; I could not say less of your workmanship.

Very respectfully, your obedient servant,
FRANCIS O. J. SMITH.

MASSACHUSETTS.

FIRE AT NORTHAMPTON.

NEW YORK, August 22, 1862.

Messrs. Herring & Co., No. 251 Broadway:

GENTLEMEN — In the latter part of June last our hoop skirt and pocket-book manufactory, at Northampton, Mass., was entirely destroyed by fire. Your Patent Champion Safe, which was in the center of the building, had all our books, papers, &c., intrusted to its care; and, though the safe was bulged and warped outside, and showed strong evidence of the heat, the inside was in good order, and no damage done except to the binding of the books. We had the safe repaired at a small expense, and now consider it good for another fire.

ARMS & BARDWELL.

CONNECTICUT.

THE GREAT FIRE IN MERIDEN, CONN., MARCH 8, 1864.

HOME BANK, WEST MERIDEN, CONN., March 10, 1864.

Messrs. Herring & Co.:

GENTLEMEN—On the night of March 8th our drug-store was totally consumed by fire. The stock of drugs and chemicals was entirely destroyed. The only things we saved were the contents of our Herring's Patent Champion Safe, which was exposed to an intense heat, notwithstanding which our books, papers, insurance policies, money, and a gold watch were taken out in excellent order. We shall need a new safe soon, and will ship the old one to you, and you can allow what it is worth in exchange.

Yours, &c., HART & FOOTE,
Druggists.

ANOTHER IN SAME FIRE, REMOVED THIRTY DAYS THEREAFTER.

MERIDEN, CONN., May, 1864.

Messrs. Herring & Co.:

GENTLEMEN—At the time of the great fire in this place on the night of the 8th of March I had in use one of your celebrated safes. I succeeded in removing all my books and papers, except a memorandum book, which I left in the safe, and the safe remained in the building in the hottest part of the fire. On opening it, thirty days after, I found the writing all perfect, which satisfied our people that your safes are what you recommend them to be—fire-proof. You will please send me another for my private house.

Yours truly, C. H. COLLINS.

ANOTHER LARGE FIRE IN MERIDEN.

WEST MERIDEN, June 24, 1865.

Messrs. Herring & Co., New York :

GENTLEMEN—In answer to your inquiries we would say that the Herring's Patent Champion Safe we bought from you was in our manufacturing establishment on the evening of its destruction by fire, on the 31st of May last. The building was large, and the fire destroyed everything in it except the contents of your safe. The safe bears the marks of a very severe roasting, but has fully and faithfully sustained your reputation, preserving all the books, money, insurance policies, and other valuable papers it contained, in such good order as to be again ready for further use.

Truly yours, J. WILCOX & CO.,
Balmoral Skirt Manufacturers.

GREAT FIRE IN NEW HAVEN.

NEW HAVEN, August 30, 1864.

Messrs. Herring & Co. :

GENTLEMEN— On the 20th instant there was a very destructive fire in this city, burning the carriage manufactory corner of Chapel and Hamilton streets, and also our machine shop. We, fortunately, were provided with one of your Champion Safes, and although the fire was so hot that iron melted and run down on the safe, and the iron casters melted off, the contents, consisting of valuable books, papers, and fifteen hundred dollars in Treasury notes, besides other bills, amounting in all to two thousand dollars, were preserved without injury. As soon as our main building is completed we shall want another safe of a larger size.

M. & T. SAULT,
Engine and Tool Builders, corner Chapel and Wallace streets.

Plate No. 2.

SIZE No. 5½.

19 in. high,
19 in. wide, } Inside.
13 in. deep,

SIZE No. 6—Low.

21 in. high,
21 in. wide, } Inside.
14 in. deep,

SIZE No. 6—High.

26 in. high,
17 in. wide, } Inside.
14 in. deep,

SIZE No. 7.

26 in. high,
21 in. wide, } Inside.
15 in. deep,

LARGE FIRE AT SIMSBURY.

SIMSBURY, August 22, 1862.

Messrs. Herring & Co.:

GENTLEMEN—It will undoubtedly give you pleasure to know, as it is a fact worthy the notice of the public, that the safe we purchased of you passed through the fire which consumed our manufactory, with all its contents, on the 20th of December, 1859. Our books, papers, and money were all preserved.

Yours truly,

TOY, BICKFORD & CO.

ANOTHER FIRE IN SIMSBURY.

SIMSBURY, February 5, 1855.

S. C. Herring, Esq.:

SIR—We take pleasure in stating that the Safe we purchased of you has nobly stood the test. Our manufactory and contents were burned on the 22d of December, but our valuable books, papers, and money, *in your safe*, were preserved uninjured. We can, therefore, with confidence, recommend your safes to the public.

Yours truly,

BACON & BROTHERS.

GREAT FIRE IN NORWICH.

BURNING OF NORWICH AND WORCESTER RAILROAD DEPOT. FOUR HUNDRED THOUSAND DOLLARS IN BONDS! TWO THOUSAND DOLLARS IN CASH SAVED!!

NORWICH & WORCESTER R.R. CO.'S OFFICE,
NORWICH, July 19, 1860.

Messrs. Herring & Co., New York:

GENTLEMEN—On the morning of the 14th inst., a destructive fire entirely consumed the depot building of this company, which was two hundred feet long and sixty-one feet wide. Your safe was in the treasurer's office, on the second floor. It affords me pleasure to inform you that the safe manufactured by you, containing books and papers of the company, has proved all you ever claimed for it. The safe was full, containing a part of our most important books and papers, which were well preserved, with the writing uninjured.

Yours respectfully,

G. L. PERKINS,
Treasurer.

ANOTHER FIRE AT NORWICH.

NORWICH, November 22, 1859.

Messrs. S. C. Herring & Co., New York:

GENTLEMEN—On the morning of the 5th inst., our bleachery was destroyed by fire, in the second story of which was one of your safes. The safe fell with the burning timbers and cotton goods, and when taken out was of a white heat. On opening it, very much to our surprise and gratification, all our books and papers were found to be uninjured, after being exposed several hours to an intense heat.

MOSES PIERCE,
Agent Norwich B. & C. Co.

FIRE AT BRIDGEPORT.

BRIDGEPORT, February, 1860.

Messrs. Silas C. Herring & Co., New York:

GENTLEMEN—My large flour mills, containing five hundred thousand feet of timber, was destroyed by fire a few weeks since. I had all my books and papers in one of your safes. When it was recovered from the ruins and opened, I found them in perfect order. You can judge of the amount of heat it had by the quantity of timber burnt over it. Cast iron shafting in the building was melted into a solid mass.

Yours respectfully,

D. P. BUCKINGHAM.

GREAT FIRE IN WEST WINSTED.

WEST WINSTED, Tuesday, March 29, 1853.

Silas C. Herring :

DEAR SIR—Some seven or ten years ago, I purchased one of your safes at $110. That safe, on the night of the 25th instant, was subjected to an intense red heat in the conflagration of my three-story brick block in this place.

After the fire commenced, an occupant of the store in which the safe was broke open the window, unlocked it, and took out *his* books, but was driven back by the flames, leaving the door open.

Arriving at the scene just at this moment and learning its situation, I made an unsuccessful attempt to get to it and lock it. I then offered a reward of $100 to a daring fellow to go in and lock the the safe. He accomplished the feat, and soon after the floor fell, with the safe, into the basement. It contained papers to a large amount, the destruction of which would have been as irretrievable as bank bills. The safe was subjected to an intense heat, surrounded by a large amount of combustible materials. On removing the safe from the fire after it had somewhat subsided (the safe being still red-hot) the papers were taken out as bright as new, in the most perfect order. The wooden lining of the safe was not disfigured at all, and presented no appearance of fire. The door-plates are warped, one wheel melted, and another partly melted off. The lock, however, works well.

Respectfully yours,

E. S. WOODFORD.

RHODE ISLAND.

DESTRUCTIVE FIRE IN PROVIDENCE.

PROVIDENCE, Dec. 5, 1846.

Mr. S. C. Herring :

SIR—Yours bearing date Dec. 24 is received. The safe we purchased of you was in the second story. It fell, with the building, some twenty feet down into the cellar ; it was exposed to all the heat of the fire, without any water. It being low tide, it was impossible to obtain a sufficient quantity of water. Your safe remained in the fire till morning, when it was taken out of the cellar and opened ; the contents were in good order, with the exception of a few lockets which were stained by the steam. It contained books, watches, jewelry, &c. The interior of your safe is as good as it was when we bought it of you.

We remain yours respectfully,

STONE & WEAVER,

per GEO. H. RHODES.

FIRE AT NEWPORT.

NEWPORT, Jan. 16, 1856.

Messrs. S. C. Herring & Co. ;

GENTLEMEN—Your note of the 14th is at hand. The safe containing my papers, some plate, &c., in my house at the time of the fire, was the same purchased of you some years since. It was surrounded by the flames and lay covered by the burn-

Plate No. 3.

No. 7—Low.

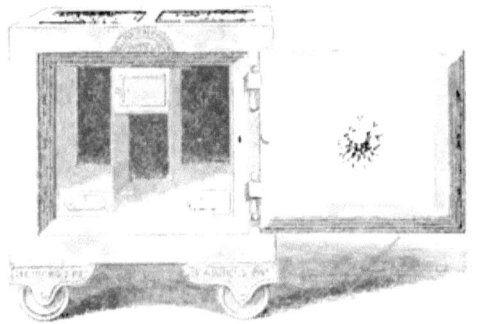

21 in. high,
26 in. wide, } Inside.
15 in. deep,

No. 8—High.

32 in. high,
22 in. wide, } Inside.
15 in. deep,

ing ruins and a solid mass of coals for the space of about twelve hours. When taken out, the lock, which is one of Hall's Patent Powder-Proof Locks, was in good condition, and all the papers contained in the safe were in good condition. The safe is damaged by having one of the hinges of the door broken, in consequence of being opened when hot.

Yours, CHAS. DEVENS.

NEW YORK CITY.

In this city alone nearly ONE HUNDRED Herring's Safes have passed through the fiery ordeal preserving their contents (amounting to millions in value) in every instance, as the following letters will show.

BURNING OF THE TRIBUNE BUILDINGS.

The destruction of this large establishment is well remembered. The entire place was burned to to the ground, and the safe in the very midst of it could not be got at until the second day after.

From the N. Y. Tribune.

"The safe has been got out and opened; the contents are in a good state of preservation. The mail-books will not even need transcribing. The pocket-books, containing money, notes, &c., and the papers, are as good as new."

From the True Sun.

"Yesterday afternoon the safe of the Tribune establishment was discovered among the ruins of the building. Is was *red-hot*. The contents, to the astonishment of all who saw them, were *uninjured!!* This nonpareil of safes had lain in its fiery bed thirty-six hours, and, judging from the appearance of its contents, would have been faithful to its trust thirty-six hours longer."

° ° ° One thing we know, however, that an ordinary single Herring's Salamander of moderate size, in which our books and money were kept, on and prior to the disastrous 5th of February last, held them safe through thirty-six hours of intense heat, in the destruction of our office by fire a year ago, and returned them to us uninjured. How much better another may do, we say not; but that this did its duty nobly we most heartily testify.—*N. Y. Tribune.*

THE GREAT FIRE IN NEW YORK, JULY 19, 1845.

From the New York Tribune, July 21, 1845.

"DESTRUCTIVE FIRE—THE BEST PORTION OF THE CITY IN RUINS—FROM $6,000,000 TO $10,000,000 WORTH OF PROPERTY DESTROYED—TERRIFIC EXPLOSION AND LOSS OF LIFE!—NEARLY 400 HOUSES DESTROYED!"

In this terrible and disastrous burning, nine "Herring's Safes" were exposed to that severe ordeal; and, although tried in that "fiery furnace," some of them for days together, yet they admirably sustained their well-earned reputation; and the interior of the safes, after their recovery from the ruins with their contents, exhibited but slight evidence of the *roasting* which they had undergone, notwithstanding the heat in many cases was so intense as to melt the iron wheels, or rollers, and other outer portions of the safes. Among those indebted to *this* safe for the preservation of their all, in that great fire, and who will bear witness now, as they experienced then, their almost fabulous properties, are the following firms, to whom the public are referred:

Messrs. CROCKER & WARREN, Messrs. CHOUTEAU & CO.,
"   D. & A. KINGSLAND & CO., Mr. HENRY LEGER,
"   MOTZ & POLITZ, Mr. J. J. LEGER,
"   SCHRAGE, KOOP & CO., And others.

In evidence of their great strength and the superiority of their general workmanship, it may be well to state that several of the above fell with the tumbling buildings at a distance varying from twenty to forty feet. The safe belonging to Messrs. Crocker & Warren was blown up with their building at the " great explosion," and the result was as follows :

NEW YORK, July 31, 1845.

Mr. S. C. Herring, No. 139 Water street :

SIR—We had in our store, No. 38 Broad street, one of the Patent Safes from your establishment. We recovered this safe from the ruins on Monday, 21st instant, after it had been exposed for *sixty hours*, and we found our books and papers in a good state of preservation; *every line of writing was perfectly legible;* we can, therefore, speak well of the safe manufactured by you.

Respectfully, your obedient servants,

CROCKER & WARREN.

NEW YORK, July 23, 1845.

Mr. Silas C. Herring :

It may be to your advantage to know that our books and papers, which were in one of your safes, have been recovered from the burning ruins of our store (at the great fire on the 19th instant) and found fit for use. The result is to our entire satisfaction.

SCHRAGE, KOOP & CO.

From the True Sun.

One gentleman saved $70,000 in bank-bills, notes, &c., by means of one of Herring's safes, and, in consequence, bore the destruction of his place of business with cheerfulness.

From the Morning News.

Several iron safes have been taken from the ruins, many of them so little injured that the books and papers are perfectly legible; that of Davis & Brooks is still standing on the second floor, and, though enveloped in flames, it is still in available condition. Barclay & Livingston have also saved their books and papers. We also hear that the safes are recovered of the following firms : Henry Leger, 46 Broad street; D. A. Kingsland & Co., 55 Broad street ; Motz & Politz, 63 Broad street, all genuine Salamanders, with their contents in good order. They were all sold by Herring, whose safe will now be received as an indispensable article in every counting-room and office.

BURNING OF THE CONGRESS SUGAR-HOUSE,

DUANE STREET, APRIL 2, 1848.

From the New York Tribune.

° ° ° We must not omit to add that the books and papers of the establishment, together with $600 in bank notes, were preserved unharmed by one of Herring's Safes. Mr. Harris was naturally in great anxiety lest the loss had been increased by the destruction of the contents of the safe, whose external appear-

Plate No. 4.

No. 8—Low.

30 in. high,
21 in. wide, Inside.
15 in. deep,

No. 9.

32 in. high,
27 in. wide, Inside.
15 in. deep,

ance, after it was dug out from among the ruins in the cellar, was anything but promising. It had been bruised by heavy substances falling upon it, and being subjected to a white heat, which had caused the exterior plates to swell and bulge in a very ominous manner, and entirely melted the brass knob of the door and the plate containing the maker's name. On drilling into it, for it could be opened in no other way, the contents were found *perfectly uninjured!* This is as triumphant a proof of the excellence of Mr. Herring's Safe as could be desired.

BURNING OF DENMAN'S LIME ESTABLISHMENT,

FOOT OF TWENTIETH STREET, N. Y.

NEW YORK, May, 1849.

Mr. S. C. Herring, No. 139 Water Street :

Although this may reach you rather late in the day to be of much useful service to you, yet even if our certification of the following facts can be a source of gratification to yourself, or the numbers already possessed of your safes, and to whose faithful trust they are now confiding for security, we would say that in the month of April, 1847, our lime establishment, foot of Twentieth street, North river, was destroyed by fire.

The safe which we bought of you was on the second floor of that building, and that, some time after the fire had commenced, our attention was directed to something in the second story, which seemed to have lodged upon the sleepers or rafters of the building. The moment it caught our eyes we at once recognized the safe in the very midst of the fire, and exposed to all the fury of the flames. The safe was plainly discernible, as it was *red-hot*, and, instead of an iron safe, had all the appearance of a burning coal. A short time after, the timbers gave way, and the safe fell with them, and there remained until our entire building was one heap of ruins. Upon opening it we found our books, papers, and even paper money (bank bills), *all safe and sound*.

And having so much confidence in your safe, which we now know to be fire-proof, we have placed the "same old Salamander" in the wall of our new building, sincerely believing that, should it ever be its lot to be once more placed as above described, the result will then be likewise.

(Signed,)   A. A. DENMAN & CO.

FULTON STREET FIRE.

NEW YORK, January 24, 1852.

Mr. Silas C. Herring :

SIR—It affords me much pleasure to be enabled to say that the safe which was in my store, 114 Fulton street, on the night of the 22d instant, when that building was destroyed by fire, was one of your make, and had been in use somewhere about five or six years; and although it was exposed to the most intense heat for twelve hours, so hot as to melt the name-plate, &c., yet on opening the safe, I was agreeably surprised to find all the books and papers, with a sum of money in bank-bills, uninjured—the interior wood casing, in all respects, as perfect as when new. As soon as I locate myself permanently I intend ordering of you another of your superior safes.

Yours respectfully,

JOHN L. WATKINS.

NEW YORK, January 24, 1852.

Mr. Silas C. Herring :

SIR—The store we occupied, No. 112 Fulton street, and the adjoining stores in Fulton and Dutch streets, were entirely consumed by fire on the night of the 22d instant ; and although the fire burned like a furnace, we are happy to say all our books, papers, and a considerable amount of money in bank-bills, were preserved in one of your safes, although the safe was exposed to an almost furnace heat for twelve hours. The contents were preserved beyond our expectations, and we have availed ourselves of another of your safes, which we intend to use until we can have one made to order of a larger size.

STILLWELL & MONTROSS.

GREAT FIRE CORNER NASSAU AND LIBERTY STREETS, NEW YORK.

NEW YORK, Feb. 24, 1852.

Mr. Silas C. Herring :

SIR— We take pleasure in being able to state that the safe we purchased of you some years since withstood the severe test to which it was subjected in the destruction of our store and merchandise by fire, on the night of the 28th of January, 1852 (corner Liberty and Nassau streets). The safe was recovered after remaining in the fire forty hours, and, to our surprise and gratification, the books, papers, money— and in fact, all the contents of the safe— were uninjured, and we are now using the same set of books. Therefore, in justice to you, we make this statement, and add our indorsement to the fame of your Salamander.

FISHERS & ROBINSON.

From the New York Herald, Jan. 30, 1852.

About nine o'clock last evening Lockwood & Co. reached their safe, which was at the time almost *red-hot*; the brass trimmings were all melted off the outside, but on opening the safe the books were found to be uninjured.

The safe was one of Herring's, which Messrs Lockwood & Co. purchased several years since.

LARGE FIRE CORNER BROADWAY AND DEY STREETS, MARCH 26, 1852.

NEW YORK, April 7, 1852.

Mr. Silas C. Herring :

SIR— We hereby certify that we had one of Herring's Safes in use at the time of the burning of our store, Nos. 5 and 7 Dey street, on the night of the 26th of March last, and that our books and papers contained therein were taken from it in a good state of preservation ; many of the books being quite uninjured, and the whole of them perfectly distinct and legible, the only damage sustained being by water.

LOTTIMER & LARGE.

NEW YORK, May 3, 1852

Mr. Silas C. Herring :

SIR— In the conflagration of our store and merchandise on the night of the 26th of March last, our books, papers, and money to a considerable amount, were secured in one of your justly celebrated safes; and we are happy to state that through the fiery ordeal which it passed, it was faithful to its name and trust. In fact, we saved every dollar and dollar's worth intrusted to its care.

MERRITT, BLISS & CO.

BURNING OF THE LAW BUILDINGS, N. Y.

NEW YORK, Feb. 16, 1853.

Mr. Silas C. Herring :

SIR—We deem it a duty to hand you a certificate of the fact that the entire contents of the safe bought of you were preserved uninjured, after remaining twelve hours in the fire, which destroyed the building occupied by us, No. 77 Nassau street, on the night of the 3d instant. The books, papers, and money were as perfect as when put into the safe, all the watch movements were in running order and some of them in motion.

J. DUCOMMIN & SON,
Watch Case Makers and Importers.

DESTRUCTION OF THE PEARL STREET HOUSE, NEW YORK.

From the Courier and Enquirer, Aug. 25, 1853.

TRIAL OF A SAFE.—One of Herring's Safes, owned by Messrs. Tilton & Molony, was exposed to the late fire by which the Pearl Street House was destroyed. A portion of the books were removed during the progress of the fire, but before the valuable papers were rescued the attempt had to be relinquished, and the safe afterward fell from the second floor to the cellar; the outer door had been left open, being broken off in the fall. The inside door was fortunately locked, and, notwithstanding the loss of the outer door and the long exposure to an intense heat, the papers were taken out uninjured.

ANOTHER OF HERRING'S SAFES TAKEN FROM THE PEARL STREET FIRE.

Mr. Silas C. Herring :

SIR—The safe I bought from you about twelve months since, and which has been exposed to the fire at the Pearl Street House on the 23d ult., is now rescued from the ruins, and I will thank you to send for it to have it repaired and a new foot put on, which was broken by carelessness in digging it out. I am happy to say that the books and papers were taken out in a state of *perfect preservation*.

I remain yours respectfully,
JOHN MAYER,
86 *Pearl street.*

THE FIRE IN GREENWICH STREET.

NEW YORK, Aug. 24, 1853.

Mr. Silas C. Herring :

SIR— I cannot too highly express the satisfaction your Superior Fire-Proof Safe has given me. All my books, papers, and evidences of debt were preserved uninjured ; and although the fire last night destroyed the stock and store occupied by me, yet the bank bills lying loose in the drawers of the safe were as perfect as when put in circulation.

Yours truly, S. S. REMSEN,
Dealer in Boots and Shoes, cor. of Vesey and Greenwich streets.

THE GREAT FIRE IN FULTON AND NASSAU STREETS—THE BURNING OF FOWLER'S BUILDINGS.

NEW YORK, Nov. 2, 1853.

Mr. S. C. Herring :

SIR—It affords us pleasure to say that the safe we purchased of you, and which was in our office in Fowler's Buildings, corner Nassau and Fulton streets, at the time of its destruction by fire, on Sunday morning last, has this day been taken from the ruins, where it has lain for more than *seventy-two hours ;* and, on opening it, we find all our books, papers, jewelry, and a considerable sum of money in bank bills, in a state of preservation that gives us entire satisfaction. We have the utmost confidence in your safes, and shall want another as soon as we can arrange the plan.

SALISBURY & ARROWSMITH.

BURNING OF THE EMPIRE IRON WORKS.

NEW YORK, November 18, 1853.

Mr. S. C. Herring:

SIR—The safe bought of you about two years since was in our office at the destruction of the "Empire Iron Works," on the morning of the 17th inst., and we are happy to say that our books, papers, and money in bank bills, were preserved to our entire satisfaction. The safe was exposed to an intense heat for about *twenty-seven hours*; the castors, brass plates, &c., melted off, and yet a valuable *gold watch* was taken out perfect and in *good time-keeping order*. We shall not be without another of your safes, and intend to call and select one early in the morning.

SLOAN & LEGGETT,
Empire Iron Works, Foot of East Twenty-fifth street.

STILL ANOTHER TESTIMONY OF A SAFE HAVING PASSED THROUGH TWO FIRES TRIUMPHANTLY.

NEW YORK, November 2, 1853.

Mr. S. C. Herring:

SIR—At the recent fire which destroyed Fowler's Buildings in Fulton street, my office was burnt out, but fortunately I had one of your safes, which contained all my stock of watches, watch movements, &c., &c., all of which were taken from the safe after the fire not damaged, except by the water unavoidably admitted at the sides of the door. This safe is also the same one that preserved my property once before at the fire No. 75 Nassau street, and which I have since used without having it refilled.

J. DUCOMMIN, 30 *Courtlandt street.*

THE GREAT FIRE IN SPRUCE STREET.

HERRING'S SAFES AGAIN TRIUMPHANT.

NEW YORK, March 6, 1854.

S. C. Herring, Esq.:

DEAR SIR—I hold it a duty which I owe to you and to the public to state that the safe I purchased of you about two years ago was the means of preserving uninjured a large amount of evidences of debt, money, &c., exposed for several hours to a tremendous heat, during the fire on Sunday morning last, in which the publication office of Thompson's *Bank Note Reporter*, No. 12 Spruce street, was entirely consumed. The safe was dug out of the ruins this day; and, on opening it, the contents, embracing notes of hand, bank-bills, policies of insurance, &c., were found to have sustained no injury other than being slightly discolored by steam. The only loss of papers and books I sustained arose from the fact that the safe was not large enough to contain them all, and those left out from this cause were destroyed. At my earliest convenience I shall call at your warehouse and select a safe of a larger size, so that hereafter I may have ample room as well as perfect security.

Very respectfully,

PLATT ADAMS, *Agent.*

STILL ANOTHER VOICE FROM THE SPRUCE STREET FIRE.

NEW YORK, March 9, 1854.

S. C. Herring, Esq.:

DEAR SIR—It is with gratitude and pleasure that I inform you of the complete success of your celebrated safe in preserving my mail-books, papers and accounts, deposited in it, from the destructive fire of the 5th instant, and which, after being

Plate No. 5.

SIZE A.

22 in. high,
32 in. wide,   Inside.
16 in. deep,

SIZE B.

22 in. high,
36 in. wide,   Inside.
16 in. deep,

buried in the burning ruins nearly four days, came forth without a trace of fire upon them. From this severe test I have increased confidence in the superiority of your safes over all others I have yet seen. You will greatly oblige me by sending me another "Salamander" forthwith, and hereafter I shall give myself no uneasiness as to the safety of its contents.

Yours truly,

Z. P. HATCH.

BURNING OF THE LAFARGE HOTEL, BROADWAY.

NEW YORK, April 20, 1854.

Mr. S. C. Herring:

SIR—We deem it our duty to the public and justice to yourself to state that we had one of your Patent Champion Safes in the Lafarge Hotel at the time that building was destroyed by fire; but, as the principal important books had been removed, we took but little interest to get the safe from the ruins for some six or eight weeks, when, to our surprise, we found the safe and its contents in a good state of preservation, although it had been for a long time surrounded by burning timbers.

Yours respectfully,

WRIGHT, LANIERS & CO.,
Late Proprietors of the Lafarge Hotel.

GREAT FIRE IN BROADWAY.

NEW YORK, April 27, 1854.

Mr. S. C. Herring:

SIR—It affords us pleasure to say that our books and papers were preserved without the least injury in two of your safes, at the destruction of our store, on the night of the 25th instant.

W. T. JENNINGS & CO.

ANOTHER FIRE IN FULTON STREET.

NEW YORK, February 10, 1855.

Mr. S. C. Herring:

SIR—We take much pleasure in informing you that the safe purchased of you on the 1st of January was recovered from the ruins of the fire of the 5th instant, at 140 Fulton street. Although it had been subjected to the most intense heat, and had remained in the ruins upward of sixty hours, all the books and papers were found to be in a legible condition. The bank bills were in a perfect state of preservation. We shall purchase another safe of you in a few days.

Respectfully yours,

J. M. FAIRCHILD & CO.,
Bookseller and Publishers, 109 Nassau Street.

FIRE IN HENRY STREET.

NEW YORK, March 22, 1855.

S. C. Herring, Esq.:

SIR—Our oil manufactory, No. 59 Henry street, was destroyed by fire on the morning of the 19th instant. Fortunately, we had one of your celebrated fire-proof safes, to which we are indebted for the preservation of all our books and valuable papers. We are so well pleased with the result that we shall use no other than your Patent Champion Safe in future. You are at liberty to publish this if you think proper.

Yours, &c., CARRINGTON & DOUGHERTY.

BURNING OF LILIENTHAL'S TOBACCO WAREHOUSE.

NEW YORK, Oct. 3, 1856.

Messrs. S. C. Herring & Co. :

It affords me pleasure to inform you that our books and papers were preserved in a safe purchased of you some time since.

The building in which the safe stood was consumed last night about ten o'clock, and we have just got the safe after lying in the ruins about eighteen hours, and find the contents perfect.

Yours respectfully,
C. H. LILIENTHAL,
per R. L. McGAY.

LARGE FIRE CORNER OF MURRAY STREET AND COLLEGE PLACE.

NEW YORK, Nov. 11, 1856.

Silas C. Herring & Co. :

GENTLEMEN We are happy to inform you of the preservation of our books and papers during the devastating fire of the 9th inst., by means of the iron safe made for us, by our order, during the spring of 1854. We have reason to believe that the Hall's Patent Powder-proof Lock has, on a former occasion, saved us from trouble and loss, by resisting the attempts of burglars made on it at that time.

Yours respectfully,
VAN WAGENEN, YEOMAN & CO.

FIRE IN COENTIES SLIP.

NEW YORK, Nov. 22, 1856.

S. C. Herring & Co. :

GENTLEMEN My store, No. 28 Coenties slip, was destroyed last evening by fire; my books, bonds, notes, and other valuable papers were preserved in a safe purchased from you about ten years since, after lying in the burning ruins twenty hours. I find my coupon bonds, money, and other valuable papers as perfect as when put in the safe, having no marks nor signs of fire on them.

Please send me another of your improved Patent Champion Safes as soon as convenient.

E. H. HERRICK.

FIRE IN PEARL STREET.

NEW YORK, Nov. 22, 1856.

S. C. Herring & Co. :

Our store, No. 136 Pearl street, was destroyed last night by fire, and it is a cause of congratulation to us to be able to assure you that our books and papers, and some money in bank-bills, were preserved entire in a safe bought of you some six years since. We esteem it our duty as it is a pleasure to add our testimony in favor of your safes, and request you to send us immediately one of your improved Patent Champion Safes, one size larger than our old one.

Yours respectfully,
O'SULLIVAN & FAYE.

FIRE IN MAIDEN LANE.

NEW YORK, Feb. 3, 1857.

Messrs. S. C. Herring & Co. :

At the burning of my store last night the safe I purchased of you some years since was tested, and I am happy to say that its contents, consisting of valuable jewelry, books, and papers, were preserved uninjured, with the exception of being stained; and my only regrets are that it was not more capacious, so that my whole stock of goods could have been preserved. I shall want another of your Champion Safes as soon as I can locate myself.

J. S. WHALEN.

GREAT FIRE IN STONE STREET.

NEW YORK, January 15, 1857.

Messrs. S. C. Herring & Co.:

GENTLEMEN—On the 19th ult. our store was destroyed by fire, containing a quantity of bacon and whiskey, and the heat was intense; but we have pleasure in stating that our books, &c., were preserved in the safe you furnished us two years ago. The only injury sustained was from water and steam, the safe having fallen with its face upward, and the books are all legible, and we think were as well protected as could have been expected.

Yours truly, HEWITT & CO.

FIRE IN BROAD STREET.

NEW YORK, February 12, 1857.

Messrs. S. C. Herring & Co.:

GENTLEMEN—My "Herring's Patent Champion Safe," purchased of you last November, was in the store destroyed by fire last night, No. 26 Broad street; and I am happy to say that, on opening the safe this morning, I found my books and papers in as good order as when placed in the safe.

F. A. DREYER.

FIRE IN MAIDEN LANE.

NEW YORK, February 13, 1857.

Messrs. S. C. Herring & Co.:

GENTLEMEN—The "Herring's Patent Champion Safe" I bought of you (for my principal) a few months since was in my store, No. 44 Maiden lane, when burned on the 2d instant; and I am pleased to say my books and papers were completely preserved without injury, and I wish you to send me another of the same kind.

GEORGE W. MAWSON, *Agent*.

GREAT FIRE IN MAIDEN LANE.

NEW YORK, February 18, 1858.

Messrs. S. C. Herring & Co.:

GENTLEMEN—On the night of the 17th instant my store, No. 55 Maiden lane, with my stock of merchandise, was entirely destroyed by fire. My loss, though heavy, would have been much more so, but that I was fortunate enough to have one of your Patent Champion Safes, which preserved uninjured my most valuable books, papers, and some bank-notes, after being eighteen hours exposed to a very severe and scorching flame. My old papers, &c., which I could not find room in the safe for, were intrusted to a vault in the wall; they are a mass of ashes.

Respectfully yours,
CHARLES AHRENFELDT.

FIRE IN FULTON AND ANN STREETS.

NEW YORK, January 30, 1860.

Messrs. S. C. Herring & Co.:

GENTLEMEN—The printing establishment, No. 113 Fulton and 48 Ann street, occupied by us and Robert Bonner of the *New York Ledger*, was yesterday morning consumed by fire. The stock of both concerns was totally destroyed. Our books, papers, and some hundreds of dollars in bank-bills, were in one of your Champion Safes; and after being exposed to the fiery ordeal for thirty hours, it has delivered up its contents without the loss of a single dollar. Experience teaches us we want no other safe than yours.

WYNKOOP, HALLENBECK & THOMAS.

GREAT FIRE IN BEEKMAN AND ANN STREETS.

NEW YORK, January, 1860.

Messrs. S. C. Herring & Co.:

The Herring's Safe which I purchased from you a short time since, and had in use in my office, No. 86 Ann street, at the time of the recent great fire in Beekman and Ann streets, was tested by fire, and preserved all my books, papers, and a quantity of precious stones, after remaining in the ruins for nearly five days. You will please deliver me another of large size to my present office, 124 Nassau street, and oblige
Yours truly,
JOHN R. SIMON.

BURNING OF WEST WASHINGTON MARKET.

NEW YORK, July 12, 1860.

Messrs. Herring & Co.:

GENTLEMEN—The Herring's Patent Champion Safe I purchased from you a few weeks since was most severely tested in the great fire last night that destroyed the West Washington Market, and, I am pleased to say, did its duty and sustained the character of your celebrated safe.

On taking it from the ruins this morning and opening it, I found my books and papers, and about five hundred dollars, mostly in bank bills, perfectly safe and uninjured, and shall want another safe as soon as I am again located.

HENRY BRINKER.

ANOTHER IN THE SAME FIRE.

NEW YORK, July 12, 1860.

Messrs. Herring & Co.:

GENTLEMEN— We have just recovered the Herring's Patent Champion Safe from the ruins of the West Washington Market fire, which occurred last night, and are pleased to inform you that our books, papers, and about six hundred dollars in money, which it contained, were found in perfect order. As soon as we get a new location we will call and select another of larger size.

J. & W. R. EADIE.

FIRE IN PLATT STREET.

NEW YORK, October 26, 1860.

Messrs. Herring & Co.:

GENTLEMEN - At the fire which destroyed my premises, No. 32 Platt street, on the morning of the 19th instant, we had our books, papers, and money locked up in one of your safes. The safe was in the second story at the time of the fire, and remained there until the burning of the floor caused it to tumble down with the ruins. We opened the safe the next morning, and found everything in the safe in good order. The books, papers, and money were as perfect as when put in.

J. PARDESSUS.

Plate No. 6.

No. ½—Folding Door.

31 in. high,
21 in. wide, } Inside.
16 in. deep,

No. 1—High, Folding Door.

38 in. high,
21 in. wide, } Inside.
16 in. deep,

ANOTHER IN THE SAME FIRE.

NEW YORK, October 26, 1860.

Messrs. Herring & Co.:

GENTLEMEN—At the time of the fire which destroyed my premises, No. 32 Platt street, I had in use one of your safes, which contained all my books, valuable papers, and money. The safe was exposed to an intense heat, and, on opening it, the contents were found to be in a perfect state of preservation. You will send me another one, larger size, when I get located.

Yours respectfully,

GAUDELET & GOURE.

FIRE IN FULTON STREET.

NEW YORK, February 13, 1861.

Messrs. Herring & Co.:

GENTLEMEN—I take pleasure in stating that the Herring's Safe which I purchased from you about eight years ago was exposed to the great fire in Fulton street, early on the morning of the 8th instant. The safe was well scorched, but the books, papers, &c., were in a perfect state of preservation, and I am so well satisfied that I order a new safe of you, to be delivered forthwith.

WILLIAM ADAMS,
No. 152 Chambers street.

FIRE ON UNION SQUARE.

NEW YORK, March 16, 1861.

Messrs. Herring & Co.:

GENTLEMEN—A safe of your manufacture was bought from you for Holland Lodge No. 8, A. Y. M. It was in our lodge room at No. 8 Union place, on Thursday night, the 14th instant, when that building was destroyed by fire. The safe fell through to the first floor as the building burned down, and I have just got at it and opened it this morning. The safe contained the books, records, warrants, and jewelry of the lodge, which were all taken out saved, having passed through the fiery ordeal successfully. The result must be as gratifying to yourselves as pleasant to us to find safely preserved many things of much value, which, had they been burned, could never have been replaced.

I am, very respectfully, yours, &c.

A. W. KING,
Secretary of Holland Lodge No. 8.

FIRE ON BROADWAY.

NEW YORK, March 19, 1861.

Messrs. Herring & Co.:

GENTLEMEN—I was the fortunate owner of one of your safes on the night of Saturday, March 16, when my store in the building No. 56 Broadway, was destroyed by fire. The safe contained my books of account, valuable papers, &c., and, when we opened it next day, the contents were found all safe and uninjured.

HENRY E. HART,
Cap Manufacturer.

FIRE IN NASSAU STREET.

NEW YORK CITY, 114 Nassau street, March 30, 1861.

Messrs. Herring & Co.:

GENTLEMEN—We have just opened our safe of your make that was in the fire this morning in Nassau street, and are happy to say that the books, papers, money, bills and gold-dust are all safe; and we consider this another test that will add to your reputation as safe-makers.

ELLES, STARR & CO.

3

MORE SAFES! FROM THE GREAT FIRE IN FULTON AND PEARL STREETS, JANUARY 26, 1862. $10,000 SAVED.

GENERAL OFFICE, NEW HAVEN STEAMBOAT CO.,
NEW YORK, January 28, 1862.

Messrs. Herring & Co., No. 251 Broadway :

GENTLEMEN—We had one of your Patent Champion Safes in the recent extensive fire, corner of Fulton and Pearl streets, on the 26th instant. The safe was in the third story of the Fulton Bank Building, and fell with the ruins to the cellar. It was taken from the ruins after *thirty-six hours'* exposure, and was *red hot*. It contained our books and papers, a considerable amount in bank-notes, and about ten thousand dollars in Treasury notes and other securities, all of which we found in good order and unscathed.

Respectfully yours,
HENRY I. WRIGHT.

STILL ANOTHER.

NEW YORK, January 27, 1862.

Messrs. Herring & Co.:

GENTLEMEN—It is with pleasure we inform you that we were the owners of one of your safes on the night of the disastrous fire, corner of Pearl and Fulton streets. The safe was in the third story of No. 273 Pearl street, and passed through the fire, falling with the ruins, from which we recovered it after being thirty-six hours in the fire. It contained all our books and papers, which were perfectly preserved from fire, being only damaged by water in cooling off the safe.

Yours respectfully,
HARTMAN & LOWEI,
Druggists.

AND ANOTHER.

NEW YORK, January 28, 1862.

Messrs. Herring & Co.:

GENTLEMEN—At the late destructive fire, corner of Pearl and Fulton streets, on the 26th instant, my books, papers, and money were all locked in one of your safes, which was situated in the second story of the building No. 269 Pearl street. The safe was subject to great heat, and was recovered from the ruins this afternoon, after being exposed for more than two days. It gives me pleasure to say that the entire contents of the safe are unharmed by fire, and everything is preserved beyond my expectations.

Yours respectfully,
JOHN ROWE.

FIRE IN DUANE STREET.

NEW YORK, April 19, 1862.

Messrs. Herring & Co. :

GENTLEMEN—At the destructive fire on the 9th instant, at No. 69 Duane street, your safe, containing my books, valuable papers, &c., was in the second story of the building and exposed to great heat. When taken out of the ruins and opened we found the contents well preserved and perfectly free from damage, excepting that the covers of the books were loosened by the steam.

DAVID STIRRATT.

FIRE IN FRONT STREET.

NEW YORK, May 31, 1862.

Messrs. Herring & Co.:

GENTLEMEN On the 31st of March last, the store No. 111 Front street, which we occupied, was consumed by fire. The safe we purchased of you some years ago was in the office on the second floor, where everything was burned. The contents of the safe were uninjured.

We have been making inquiries, from time to time, since, for the purpose of ascertaining what safes afford the *best* security against fire, and have come to the conclusion to continue the use of yours, as being, in our opinion, the most reliable for that purpose.

Yours truly,

CARTWRIGHT & HARRISON.

BURNING OF ALTHAUSE BUILDING, NEW YORK.

NEW YORK, November 17, 1862.

Messrs. Herring & Co.:

GENTLEMEN In answer to your inquiries in regard to my safe, I would answer that it was one of your make, and has been worth to me many times its cost. It was in my office in the second story of the Althause Building, corner of Houston and Greene streets, on Saturday evening, 15th instant, when that structure was totally destroyed by fire. I found it in the ruins this morning, with evidence on the outside of its having been subjected to great heat. The plate and knob were melted off, and, as it would not unlock, I was obliged to force it open, when, to my great gratification, my books, papers, insurance policies, money, &c., came forth without further damage than was caused by steam, and with hardly the smell of fire upon them.

Yours truly,

A. CARR.

ANOTHER IN THE SAME FIRE.

NEW YORK, November 18, 1862.

Messrs. Herring & Co.:

GENTLEMEN—The Herring's Safe which I lately purchased contained my books and papers at the time my establishment was destroyed in the fire corner of Houston and Greene streets, on the night of the 15th instant.

The safe was dug out this yesterday, and, on opening it, I found the books and papers in a good state of preservation. You will please send for the old safe, and when I get into my new office I shall want one of a larger size.

JOHN THOMSON.

GREAT FIRE CORNER FULTON AND GOLD STREETS, NEW YORK.

NEW YORK, January 7, 1863.

Messrs. Herring & Co., No. 251 Broadway:

GENTLEMEN—At the recent extensive fire on the night of the 1st instant, which burned ten buildings, our place of business, No. 75 Fulton street, was entirely destroyed. We had a safe of your manufacture in the back part of our store, and, consequently, in the very center of the conflagration.

The safe was dug out this afternoon, and was hot when we reached it, though it is now the sixth day since the fire took place. The safe contained our insurance policies, valuable papers, money, and a large amount of jewelry. The papers and money are as good as when put in; nothing is injured but the jewelry, which is stained and was broken in the fall of the safe. The result gives us great satisfaction, and we can pronounce your safes truly fire-proof, and further say that we want another safe of your make, and will trust no other.

DACORSI & CO.

Plate No. 8.

No. 2--Low, Folding Door.

31 in. high,
32 in. wide,   } Inside.
16 in. deep,

No. 3—Folding Door.

41 in. high,
32 in. wide,   } Inside.
17 in. deep,

FIRE IN WASHINGTON STREET, NEW YORK.

NEW YORK, Jan. 12, 1863.

Messrs. Herring & Co., New York:

GENTLEMEN—It is gratifying to us to bear testimony to the value of your fire-proof safes, and that they are truly what they are called. As our valuable books and papers were saved uninjured in one of your safes at the late fire in Washington street, on the night of the 24th ultimo, our confidence is confirmed, and with the new one recently purchased we rest safely without fear of fire.

WILLIAM J. STITT & CO.

GREAT FIRE IN DUANE STREET.

NEW YORK, Jan. 25, 1864.

Messrs Herring & Co., No. 251 Broadway, N. Y.:

GENTLEMEN The two safes of your manufacture which we had in use on the night of the 16th instant, at the destructive fire in Duane street, have given us great satisfaction and been the means of preserving our books, policies of insurance, and valuable papers, and everything trusted to their keeping. Owing to the condition of the surrounding walls, it was impossible for the workmen to dig for the safes until Friday, the 23d instant—the sixth day after the fire. The large safe, when it was reached, was cut into, as it could not be opened otherwise, and our books and papers were found to be in excellent order—nothing injured but the binding, effected by the steam. The small safe was found in the ruins and was opened by cutting into it, like the other. We are happy to say that its entire contents were perfectly preserved, and it gives us much pleasure to add our indorsement to the well-earned reputation of your Fire-proof Safes.

We are yours, &c.,

AUFFMORDT, HESSENBERG & CO.

BURNING OF THE BLOCK KNOWN AS THE EMPIRE WORKS, TWENTY-FOURTH AND TWENTY-FIFTH STREETS.

NEW YORK, Feb. 18, 1864.

Messrs Herring & Co.:

GENTLEMEN—On the night of the 6th of February the large six-story building known as the Empire Works, on Twenty-fourth and Twenty-fifth streets, near the East river, was wholly destroyed by fire. I had in my office one of your Fire-proof Safes, which has this day been dug out from the ruins and opened. Everything inside—books, papers, and money—were all preserved in good order; and I would like you to take the safe to your factory, and as soon as I get located I will make arrangements for a new safe.

In the same office was a safe manufactured by Chamberlain & Co., the contents of which were entirely consumed.

Respectfully,

SAMUEL LEGGETT.

FIRE IN ANN STREET.

NEW YORK, April 22, 1864.

Messrs. Herring & Co., New York:

GENTLEMEN I had one of your safes, Herring's Patent, in the third story of my building, No. 45 Ann street, which was five stories high at the time it was destroyed by fire. The safe fell with the building and remained until everything but your safe was destroyed. It was taken out this morning, and on opening it I am happy to say all its contents—books, papers, &c.—are perfectly preserved.

WM. McKENZY.

BURNING OF THE CAMDEN AND AMBOY RAILROAD DEPOT.

NEW YORK, July 12, 1864.

Messrs. Herring & Co.:

GENTLEMEN—Two iron safes of medium size made by you for this company were in the second story of their office, on Pier No. 1 North river, during the conflagration by which the pier was entirely destroyed of its buildings and freight yesterday morning, a large steamer being also destroyed. The safes were opened in my presence yesterday, and the contents, consisting of valuable papers, books, banknotes, &c., were found to be in good order, with the slight exception of spoiling of the binding of the books. The books when rebound will be as good as new. This may be considered a very fiery ordeal for the safes with a satisfactory result.

Yours respectfully,

A. DECKER,
Cashier.

LARGE FIRE IN BROADWAY.

NEW YORK, September 19, 1864.

Messrs. Herring & Co.:

GENTLEMEN—Our store was destroyed by fire this morning about three o'clock, and our books and papers were in one of your safes—"Herring's Patent"—which, on being opened, we found everything all safe and in good order, and are perfectly satisfied that your safes are what they are designed for—good security against fire.

Yours truly,

BANGS, MERWIN & CO.

FIRE IN PEARL STREET.

NEW YORK, November 25, 1863.

Messrs. Herring & Co., No. 251 Broadway:

GENTLEMEN—My store, No. 76 Pearl street, was destroyed by fire on the night of the 10th instant, with all its contents. The "Herring's Patent Safe," which I bought of you, containing my books, insurance policies, valuable papers, &c., was taken out of the ruins on the 14th instant. Everything in the safe was well preserved and gives me perfect satisfaction. I am using the same books which I held so safely through the fire. I wish you would send me another, same size and kind, to my new office at No. 83 Pearl street, and allow me for the old one whatever it may be worth.

Respectfully yours,

WM. J. SCHIDEL.

ANOTHER FIRE IN BROADWAY.

NEW YORK, December 14, 1863.

Messrs. Herring & Co., No. 251 Broadway :

GENTLEMEN—At the recent destructive fire on the night of the 8th instant my store, No. 356 Broadway, with its entire contents, was destroyed. Fortunately my books and papers were locked up in one of your Champion Safes, which we recovered from the ruins the day following. It is a great satisfaction for me to add that my books, papers, policies of insurance, money—and indeed everything in the safe—was in good order and not in the least harmed by fire.

Respectfully,

J. LAGOWITZ.

ANOTHER IN SAME FIRE.

NEW YORK, December 15, 1863.

Messrs. Herring & Co. :

GENTLEMEN—The Herring's Patent Champion which I purchased from you was in my office on the second floor of No. 356 Broadway, on the night of the 8th instant, when that building was destroyed by fire. The safe was in the back part of the building and was exposed to the hottest part of the fire. It fell with the destruction of the building and was dug from the ruins on the afternoon of the day following. When it was opened the interior was well preserved and all my books and papers found in as good and legible condition as when they were put in.

Truly yours,

PHILO SCOFIELD.

FIRE IN THE BOWERY.

NEW YORK, December 22, 1863.

Messrs. Herring & Co.:

GENTLEMEN—We take great pleasure in bearing witness to the fire-proof qualities of your safes, one of which—a small size—passed through the fire at the burning of our store, No. 295 Bowery, on the night of December 21st. A large amount of combustibles surrounded the safe, such as lard, bacon, &c. After some twelve hours we succeeded in removing the safe from the ruins and found our books, insurance policies, &c., in a good state of preservation. The books, with rebinding, will still answer for further use.

Respectfully, &c.,

KELSEY & CADY.

GREAT FIRE IN BEEKMAN STREET.

NEW YORK, December 24, 1864.

Messrs. Herring & Co., No. 251 Broadway:

GENTLEMEN—It has been our misfortune to have our place of business, at No. 55 Beekman street, entirely destroyed by the fire of last night. The Herring Safe we purchased from you some time ago, was in our office on the third floor of the building, which contained our papers, &c. We succeeded in reaching it this afternoon, and are happy to say that we found its entire contents, consisting of books, papers, insurance policies, bank-bills, &c., &c., all in a well-preserved condition; no injury whatever, except the leather which is curled by the steam from the fire-proof composition.

JOHN WOLF.
JOHN B. DASH.

BURNING OF THE AMERICAN MUSEUM.

LETTER FROM MR. BARNUM.

NEW YORK, July 14, 1865.

Messrs. Herring & Co.:

GENTLEMEN—Though the destruction of the American Museum has proved a serious loss to myself and the public, I am happy to verify the old adage, that "It's an ill wind that blows nobody good," and consequently congratulate you that your well-known safes have again demonstrated their superior fire-proof qualities in an ordeal of unusual severity.

The safe you made for me some time ago was in the office of the Museum, on the second floor, back part of the building, and in the hottest of the fire.

After twenty-four hours of trial it was found among the debris, and, on opening it this day, has yielded up its contents in very good order, books, papers, policies of insurance, bank bills, all in condition for immediate use, and a noble commentary on the trustworthiness of Herring's Fire-proof Safes.

Truly yours,

P. T. BARNUM.

ANOTHER.

New York, March 21, 1866.

Messrs. Herring & Co.:

Gentlemen—At the time of the great fire which destroyed Barnum's Museum and adjoining buildings, last July, I had one of your justly celebrated safes. It was situated on the first floor of No. 216 Broadway, and was subjected to intense heat, remaining in the ruins over one week, notwithstanding which, the contents, consisting of books and valuable papers, were preserved in excellent order. It gives me much pleasure to add my testimony to the security of your safes, and trust, should I have the misfortune to be burned out again, that my books and papers may be again locked in one of your Champion Safes.

Respectfully,

GEORGE W. WHITE,
Hatter, late No. 216 Broadway.

AND ANOTHER.

New York, July 15, 1865.

Messrs. Herring & Co.:

Gentlemen As you are aware, our store was located in the building known as Barnum's Museum, when that establishment was entirely destroyed by fire. The safe of your manufacture which we had in use remained in the building and was exposed to intense heat. Our books had mostly been taken out of the safe before the fire reached us, but some valuable papers and a book or two that were left in the safe came out all right when the safe was opened. The safe was exhumed from its fiery resting-place yesterday afternoon, and, although it shows severe marks of the heat on the outside, to the surprise of all, the books, papers, &c., that remained inside and the woodwork in the safe are all found to be in a safe condition.

P. L. ROGERS' SONS.

AND ANOTHER.

New York, July 14, 1865.

Messrs. Herring & Co.:

Gentlemen - We are pleased to inform you that our insurance policies and other papers left in one of your safes have just been delivered to us all safe and in good order, after having passed through the fire which destroyed Barnum's Museum. The books were taken out of the safe before the fire reached it, and the safe closed and locked. After being in the fire for more than twenty-four hours the safe was dug out of the ruins, and the inside case, with all its contents, found to be as good as new.

Yours respectfully,

SHERWOOD & METZINGER,
No. 151 Fulton street.

YET ANOTHER.

New York, September 1, 1865.

Messrs. Herring & Co., No. 251 Broadway:

Gentlemen At the destruction of Barnum's Museum, on the 14th of July last, it was my misfortune to be located in the third story of the adjoining property on Broadway and Fulton streets, and all the effects of my office, together with one of your patent safes, were enveloped in that destructive fire. The safe fell from its position on the third floor and was not recovered from the ruins until nearly a month afterward. Yesterday it was opened, and it is a source of much gratification to assure you that the "Herring's Safe" has proved fire-proof indeed. Although well roasted outside, and showing the most severe marks of the heat, all

Plate No. 9.

No. 3½—High, Folding Door.

50 in. high,
32 in. wide, } Inside.
17 in. deep,

No. 3½—Low, Folding Door.

39 in. high,
39 in. wide, } Inside.
17 in. deep,

my books, papers, and everything in the safe were in good order, there being no evidence of damage on any portion of the contents except the book-bindings, which were affected by the steam. Every line of writing and every scrap of paper was perfect.

Truly yours,
D. D. NASH,
late Auctioneer.

BURNING OF BLEECKER STREET AND FULTON FERRY CAR DEPOT.

BOOKS, PAPERS, AND MONEY PRESERVED IN HERRING'S PATENT CHAMPION SAFE.

NEW YORK, February 6, 1866.

Messrs. Herring & Co., No. 251 Broadway :

GENTLEMEN—We had a severe trial of one of your Patent Champion Safes in the entire destruction of our depot buildings on Saturday night, the 3d instant. The safe was in our office in the second story of the large brick building on Fourteenth street, and exposed to a great body of flame, from the large amount of hay and other combustible material contained in the burning stables.

We got the safe out next day and opened it. The books, papers, money in bank bills, were all well preserved, nothing being injured except the leather bindings.

JACOB SHARP,
President of the Bleecker Street and Fulton Ferry Railroad Company.

THE GREAT FIRE CORNER OF BROADWAY AND BARCLAY STREET, APRIL 6, 1866.

BURNING OF BANG'S BUILDING.

NUMBER ONE.

NEW YORK, April 6, 1866.

Messrs. Herring & Co., No. 251 Broadway :

GENTLEMEN—The Herring Patent Safe we bought of you a few years ago has just been dug out from the ruins of the recent extensive fire, corner of Broadway and Barclay street. Our building, No. 231 Broadway, where the fire originated, was entirely burnt out, and we had barely time to escape with our lives. The safe was exposed to intense heat, yet we are happy to inform you that everything it contained—books, papers, and money—are good as new.

H. J. BANG,
No. 231 Broadway.

NUMBER TWO.

NEW YORK, April 9, 1866.

Messrs. Herring & Co., No. 251 Broadway :

GENTLEMEN—The large safe of your manufacture which we had in use at the time of the destructive fire, corner of Broadway and Barclay street, has been rescued from the site of our late building and opened this afternoon. It affords us great satisfaction to say to you that we find our books, valuable papers, and the entire contents preserved in good condition, nothing injured, except the leather covers of the books being steamed.

FAIRCHILD, WALKER & CO.,
Rooms 6 and 7, No. 229 Broadway.

NUMBER THREE.

NEW YORK, April 9, 1866.

Messrs. Herring & Co., No. 251 Broadway:

GENTLEMEN—I this morning recovered from the ruins of the fire, corner of Broadway and Barclay street, the safe purchased of you some years since, and, to my entire satisfaction, found the contents in a perfect state of preservation. The safe had lain in the ruins since Friday morning, and was in the hottest part of the fire. I shall in the future feel safe to trust any amount of property to your safe.

J. M. ROBERTSON.

NUMBER FOUR.

NEW YORK, April 16, 1866.

Messrs. Herring & Co., No. 251 Broadway:

GENTLEMEN— In the recent extensive fire, corner of Broadway and Barclay street, the premises which I occupied were entirely destroyed. The Herring's Safe which I purchased from you was in my office on the second floor, and fell with the ruins to the cellar. It has since been exhumed and opened, and I find all its contents, consisting of books of account, valuable papers, &c., &c., in excellent condition. Everything in the safe is as good for use as before the fire.

Respectfully,

M. COURTRIGHT.

ANOTHER GREAT FIRE THE SAME NIGHT,

CORNER BROADWAY AND FULTON STREET.

NUMBER ONE.

NEW YORK, April 9, 1866.

Messrs. Herring & Co., No. 251 Broadway:

GENTLEMEN— In the destructive conflagration of the 6th instant it was our misfortune to be located on the lower floor of the five story building No. 202 Broadway The large safe of your manufacture which we had in use was in the back part of the building more than one hundred and fifty feet from Broadway, difficult to reach with water, and exposed to the hottest of the fire.

We got at it on Saturday afternoon, and found the knobs and plates melted off, and were obliged to cut the doors open, when, to our great satisfaction, we found our books, papers, policies of insurance, money—and indeed everything in the safe—in first-rate condition.

Respectfully yours,

KNAPP & SNIFFEN.

NUMBER TWO.

NEW YORK, April 9, 1866.

Messrs. Herring & Co.:

GENTLEMEN—I have just opened my Herring's Patent Safe, which has lain among the embers of the Broadway and Fulton street fire since Friday morning, the 6th instant. The safe was in my office, on the third floor, and was in the hottest part of the fire. Notwithstanding the fall and great heat endured, the safe has been true to its name and trust, and faithfully sustained the reputation of your house.

All my books and papers contained in the safe are in as good condition as before the fire, except the slight damage occasioned by the steam which comes from the fire-proof filling.

JOHN B. BEHRMANN.

NUMBER THREE.

NEW YORK, April 7, 1866.

Messrs. Herring & Co. :

GENTLEMEN—We are pleased to be able to add our testimony in favor of one of your safes that we had in our office at the time of the great fire, yesterday, on Broadway and Fulton street, and would say, for the benefit of the public and in justice to you, that all our books, papers, etc., were taken out to-day in good order, after the safe had been exposed to an intense heat.

HENRY SIEDE,

No. 202 Broadway.

NUMBER FOUR.

NEW YORK, April 7, 1866.

Messrs. Herring & Co. :

GENTLEMEN—I am happy to say that, having recovered my safe (one of your make) from the ruins of our store, No. 150 Fulton street, which was destroyed by fire yesterday, and having opened it, I find all its contents, consisting of books, papers, money, bonds, and Government stocks, belonging to myself, and others intrusted to us for safe keeping, perfectly safe and uninjured. This safe stood an extraordinary heat and proves the excellency of your safes.

C. C. RICHMOND.

BURNING OF THE ACADEMY OF MUSIC—HERRING'S SAFE IN THE MIDST OF THE FLAMES.

NEW YORK, May 28, 1866.

Messrs. Herring & Co. :

GENTLEMEN—The destruction of the Academy of Music—the largest building in the city, involving with it the destruction of a half a block of buildings—has been a severe trial of the fire-resisting quality of your safe.

Your manufacture has again demonstrated its superior usefulness. Situated in the eastern part of the building, where the great body of flame was swept by the force of a strong wind, the Herring's Safe was the only remnant of that vast edifice which the fire could not conquer.

We found the safe among the ruins a few days ago, and have since opened it, finding the whole interior book-case, with its contents, in a wonderful state of preservation. Some few papers that fell against the door were discolored, but everything else was in perfect order.

Truly yours,

EMIL RULLMANN.

BURNING OF HEGEMAN & CO.'S DRUG STORE.

NEW YORK, August 23, 1866.

Messrs. Herring & Co. :

GENTLEMEN—We are happy to inform you that, in the recent destructive fire at our store, 203 Broadway, our books, valuable papers, cash, &c., were all perfectly preserved in one of your Champion Safes ; and, although the heat received so affected it that we were obliged to cut it to get it open, everything was in as perfect condition as before the fire.

Very respectfully yours,

HEGEMAN & CO.

GREAT FIRE IN WEST AND WASHINGTON STREETS.

NEW YORK, Oct. 23, 1866.

Messrs. Herring, Farrel & Sherman, 251 Broadway:

GENTS—At the recent destructive fire in West and Washington streets, on 15th inst., we were the owners of one of your Herring's Patent Champion Safes, which was filled with books and valuable papers, not only those of our own, but two other concerns in which we are interested. The Safe was got out of the ruins a few days ago, and is the only article not consumed in our building; all else is "clean gone."

On opening we were pleased to find all our books, papers, and entire contents of the Safe well preserved; some of the backs of the books are drawn by the steam, but this is the only mark of the severe trial to which they have been exposed.

J. C. BAXTER & SONS,

308 West street, N. Y.

NEW YORK STATE.

GREAT FIRE AT SAG HARBOR, NOVEMBER 13, 1845.

The fire which devastated this place in November, 1845, can never be forgotten—destroying, at the very verge of winter, almost the entire business portion of the place. Over one hundred buildings, including the bank, were leveled with the ground.

[*Extract from a letter from Mr. Adams, President of the Suffolk County Bank, Sag Harbor, to John Thompson, Esq., Wall street.*]

We have recovered our safe from the burning ruins of our banking-house, and succeeded in getting it open, and find all safe, even to the bills. I shall send it up by the first vessel, and wish Herring to send me another; the same size, with Jones' lock on it, the same as this was. It takes Herring's Safe and Jones' Lock to be *fire* and *burglar-proof*.

ANOTHER.

SAG HARBOR, SUFFOLK CO., L. I., NEW YORK, November 20, 1845.

We had in our store, at the time of its destruction at the great fire in Sag Harbor, on the 13th November, 1845, one of Herring's Safes. This safe fell into the cellar and remained there until the store and contents were entirely consumed. The safe was exposed to great heat, produced by the oil, candles, drugs, &c., stored in our cellar; and, upon opening it, we found our books, papers, and several hundred dollars in bank-bills, in good order. We take great pleasure in making this statement to the public, and in recommending them to *Herring's Safes* as fully entitled to their confidence. We have purchased another of the same kind, and we never intend to be without one of these *genuine* Salamander Safes.

G. & H. HUNTING.

GREAT FIRE IN ALBANY, MAY 15, 1848.

This was the second series of great fires with which Albany city appears at this time to have been scourged. In this fire a large number of warehouses were destroyed.

Plate No. 10.

No. 4—Folding Door.

50 in. high,
38 in. wide, } Inside.
17 in. deep,

Mr. S. C. Herring:

Sir—Thinking it due to you, and a precautionary measure to all business persons, I hereby certify, that I had in the late fire, 15th instant, in my store, one of your safes in the most exposed part of the fire—there being a large quantity of oil directly in front and overhead, which, when on fire, created an intense heat, heating the safe to such a degree that I did not open it for forty-eight hours after the fire, and then, in parts of the safe, it was quite warm; and what was more satisfactory, my papers, &c., were all perfect, with the exception of being a little smoked, caused, I think, by oil running on the safe.

R. BORTLE.

I can cheerfully certify to the above, and further, that I had one of the same kind of safes in Mr. Thorn's store at the same time, where I kept my papers and books, and the result of mine was the same as the above.

J. O. HAIGHT.

I hereby certify that I purchased of Mr. S. C. Herring both of the above safes, and I consider it poor economy in any business man not to have one of the same make.

S. T. THORN.

ANOTHER GREAT FIRE AT ALBANY, AUGUST 17.

FIVE HUNDRED BUILDINGS IN ASHES

ALBANY, August 29, 1848.

S. C. Herring, Esq.:

Sir—I hereby certify that the accompanying safe is the one Alderman Thorn purchased of you for me, which safe was in his store at the time he was burned out, on the 15th of May last, and so well preserved my books and papers at that time.

I then put it in my office, on the second floor of my steam-engine and boiler shop, and at the great fire on the 17th instant it went through another ordeal and fell in the cellar on the coal pit, and there lay on a bed of burning coal for forty-eight hours after the fire; when, out of curiosity more than anything else, as it was supposed that everything in it was consumed, it was got out, and the lock being sprung so as not to open easily with the key, I forced open the door, and, to my and others' utter astonishment, the books and papers that were in it were still safe and legible and could easily be copied; and the accompanying alphabet is a fair sample of the whole. I make this statement, sir, that the public may know the security in the *real* Salamander Safe.

J. O. HAIGHT.

I have copied all the necessary books and papers spoken of above without any difficulty, and hereby certify that the above statement of Mr. Haight is correct in every particular.

S. T. THORN,
Alderman Third Ward.

The alphabet herewith sent was in the safe at both fires.

ALBANY, August 17, 1848.

Silas C. Herring, Esq.:

DEAR SIR—The safe of your make which we purchased of your agent in this city, S. M. Parke, this spring, has proved of more than ordinary value to us and far superior to the other iron safes which are used. Your safe was in our warehouse and locked up, with all our books and some papers in it, when our building was burned down at the great fire in this city on the 17th.

We got at the safe and opened it this day, and found our books and papers safe, though the leather covers on the books were somewhat drawn. We had a safe, so called, of another manufacture, in the same warehouse, and find that there is not a vestige of a book or paper in it. Everything it contained was destroyed, and it was as full of old books and papers as your safe.

We return you the safe and wish a larger one made for us. The dimensions of the one we wish you to make we will send you in a few days.

By examining the old safe which we return to you, you can see what heat it was exposed to by the brass plate being melted off, and the expansion of the iron bands, &c.

Yours truly,
WM. MONTEATH & CO.

ALBANY, August 22, 1848.

S. C. Herring, Esq.:

DEAR SIR—The safe we bought of you in the spring of 1847 has been thoroughly tested by the late fire, and, we are happy to state, has more than answered our expectations.

We were unfortunately located on the pier, and, as you must have learned ere this, we had but bare time to escape with our lives before every building located there, as far north as the cut, was in flames.

Our safe stood facing the south, in the second story, and consequently faced the flames, which, with the strong south wind, made a heat almost as severe as a blast furnace and something of the same nature. Notwithstanding all this, our books and papers were preserved, so that they are all legible, and many of them as perfect as they were before the fire.

It is wonderful that it could have withstood such a violent heat with no more injury, when we know the heat to have been so powerful as to destroy the old-fashioned safes that were taken out of the stores on the pier and placed some distance from the buildings. B. S. Jones drew out his and placed it to the water's edge; still it was destroyed, while yours saved the papers and books in the hottest of the fire.

Yours respectfully,
C. W. GODDARD & CO.

P. S.—The books and papers were taken from the safe two days after the fire.

ALBANY, August 23, 1848.

Mr. S. C. Herring, Water street, New York:

DEAR SIR—We purchased one of your safes (one hundred dollar size) last fall and were much pleased with it. On the 24th of April last our store, No. 34 Green street, with all its contents, was burnt, and the fire was believed to be the hottest which ever occurred in this city, the great fire of the 17th instant excepted. Your safe, with our books and papers, lay in the burning ruins for three days; yet, when taken out, our books and papers were in as good condition as when put in the safe.

The above safe was also in the great fire of the 17th instant, at No. 382 Broadway, though the principal part of my books and papers had been removed. During the first fire, as above mentioned, the safe was very much exposed, both to the heat and the tumbling ruins. During the latter I do not think it was quite so much exposed, although it was two days before we recovered it from the midst of the ruins; yet, when taken out and opened, every book and paper was perfectly found.

I, however, do not feel disposed to risk it in a third fire, having been heated to a great degree the second time. You will, therefore, do me the favor to forward me another immediately, one size larger; and if the burnt safe is of any use to you, you may send for it.

Yours, &c.,
A. BLAIR & CO.,
Upholsterers, No. 34 Green street.

HERRING'S FIRE-PROOF SAFES.

ALBANY, September 7, 1848.

Mr. S. C. Herring:

SIR—We had one of your large size safes in our office, which was destroyed at the great fire in this city on the 17th ultimo. We removed most of the books and papers before the fire reached us, and after the building was destroyed we felt but little anxiety about the safe for some days; and, supposing, from the great heat of the burning ruins where it lay, that it must be destroyed, we made no effort to recover it.

Some twenty days after we dug it out, and, on its being opened, some letters which had been left in the safe were found as perfect as if they had not been exposed; and we have no doubt, had our books remained in the safe, they would have been preserved.

The safe was exposed to an intense heat, and had the appearance, when taken from the ruins, of being entirely destroyed. The brass plates and knobs were all melted off, and the plate and bar-iron had the appearance of having remained in a state of white heat a long time; but yet the varnish on the inside was bright and the interior book-case as good as new.

We shall want another safe soon and will send you our order as soon as we determine on the size we want.

Yours respectfully,

ELIJAH COBB & CO.

ALBANY, September 12, 1848.

Mr. S. C. Herring:

SIR—We have this day taken from the ruins of the fire, August 17, 1848, our safe, which we purchased of you some time since. We had made several previous attempts to reach it, but, the heat where it laid was so intense, we did not succeed until the rain had cooled the rubbish sufficient to allow us to work around it. The safe was quite hot when we reached it, and, from the outside appearance, we supposed it was entirely destroyed. We were very much surprised to find, upon opening it, the wood-work in good order and not burnt in the least; in fact, the varnish is not even started. There were no books or papers in the safe, yet we are satisfied, if there had been, they would have been perfectly secure. If you want the safe forwarded to you please write to us.

Yours respectfully,

M. S. WADLEY & CO.

P. S.—There has not been any water thrown upon the building from the time it caught fire, with the exception of the rain.

FIRE AT BUFFALO, FEBRUARY 3, 1847.

BUFFALO, March 19, 1847.

S. C. Herring, Esq., New York:

GENTLEMEN—We had in our store, at the time of its destruction by fire on the morning of the 3d February, 1847, one of your safes, purchased of Mr. Sidney Sheppard, agent at this place. The safe was in the fire from the time of its commencement until our entire building was consumed, and in taking it from the ruins, we are happy to state, on opening it found our books and all its contents entirely preserved. We take great pleasure in making this statement to the public, and in recommending to them Herring's Safe as fully entitled to their confidence.

HAYWOOD & NOYES.

LARGE FIRE AT BUFFALO, 1854.

BUFFALO, N. Y., December 14, 1854.

Silas C. Herring:

SIR—We roasted a Herring last night, and notwithstanding we started the scales freely, it came out triumphant. The safe was one of Herring's Patent, and was in Truscott's distillery, which was burned, and made a hot fire. We had it brought to our store this morning and cut open; books, bonds, mortgages, notes, bank-bills, and gold were all as good as new, except the covers of some of the books being a little curled by steam.

Yours respectfully,
WEEKS & PRESCOTT,
Agents.

From the Buffalo Daily Republic.

There is standing in front of the premises of Messrs. Weeks & Prescott, 81 Main street, a safe—Herring's Improved Champion—which is a curiosity to look upon. It belongs to Messrs. Truscott & Co., whose distillery was destroyed by fire on Wednesday evening. The safe was so warped and sprung by the action of the intense heat to which it had been subjected on the occasion referred to that it was impossible to unlock it, and it was brought to the establishment of W. & P. for the purpose of being opened, which, after considerable difficulty, was effected by being cut into. When opened, much to the surprise and delight of the owners, the contents (which we have personally inspected, and can vouch for the truth of what we state), consisting of a set of account books, bonds and mortgages, policies of insurance, notes, bank bills, specie, &c., were found to be in a perfect state of preservation—not the slightest signs of any unusual heat being visible in any part thereof.

LARGE FIRE IN BUFFALO, 1858.

BUFFALO, February 3, 1858.

Messrs. S. C. Herring & Co.:

GENTLEMEN—George B. Flensheim, of this city, who purchased of me one of your safes for jewelry, books, &c., had it burned in the fire of the 24th of December last, and although it was exposed to the hottest part of the fire, yet we were astonished, on opening it, that all the contents were in the most perfect state of preservation. Not even the drawers that contained his jewelry show the marks of fire in any way. The safe was unlocked with the key, and, by painting over, it will be as good as ever.

Yours truly,
JOHN WEEKS.

FIRE IN BUFFALO, 1862.

BUFFALO, N. Y., Oct. 6, 1863.

Messrs. Herring & Co.:

GENTLEMEN—On the 19th September, 1862, my grain elevator and office were destroyed by fire. I had in my office one of your Champion Safes, which contained my books, papers, and money. The safe was subjected to a most severe heat for about *thirty hours*. After removing it from the ruins and opening it, I found the contents uninjured, everything being legible and as useful for reference as any of my old books, the only injury being to the covers of the books, which came off probably from the action of the steam.

I would recommend those wishing a genuine fire-proof safe to purchase one of *your* "Iron-clads."

Yours respectfully,
CHARLES W. EVANS.

Plate No. 11.

No. 4½—Folding Door.

56 in. high,
38 in. wide, } Inside.
18 in. deep,

GREAT FIRE IN BUFFALO, SEPTEMBER 14, 1863.

BUFFALO, N. Y., Sept. 20, 1863.

Messrs. Herring & Co.:

GENTLEMEN—Our city was visited by a very destructive fire last Monday night, September 14, destroying the building in which we had our office. Our books, papers, and money were preserved in one of your fire-proof safes—this safe was, subjected to an intense heat for ten hours and has done us good service.

Respectfully yours,

PEASE & TROWBRIDGE.

ANOTHER IN SAME FIRE.

BUFFALO, September 20, 1863.

Messrs. Herring & Co.:

GENTLEMEN—I take pleasure to inform you that one of your patent safes has been the means of saving my books, papers, &c., in perfect condition, at the large fire which occurred here on Monday night, the 14th September. The safe remained in the ruins *fifteen hours*, and was subjected to so great a heat that the brass ornamental plate and knob are melted off.

Respectfully yours,

ANDREW BROWN.

FIRE AT SYRACUSE, N. Y.

SYRACUSE, October 2, 1851.

S. C. Herring, Esq. :

SIR—In November last I purchased of your agent here, Mr. Israel Hall, one of your safes, which was in my planing mill at the time it was burnt, a few days since. The building was four stories high and full of lumber, shavings, oil, and combustible materials, all of which were totally destroyed. Your safe, containing all my notes, books, and other papers, was in the midst of the fire. The next day the safe was removed from the ruins, and, on opening it, all the books and papers were in perfect order and uninjured.

E. HOLLISTER.

GREAT FIRE AT SYRACUSE.

From the Daily Standard, Syracuse, November 13, 1856.

HERRING'S PATENT CHAMPION SAFE.

One of Herring's Fire-proof Safes, sold by D. S. & S. P. Geer, of this city, passed through the ordeal of a recent fire in the First Ward of this city, and its contents came out in excellent order, as the following certificate triumphantly proves :

SALINA, November 13, 1856.

Messrs. D. S. & S. P. Geer, Agents, or to all whom it may concern :

This is to certify that the safe of S. C. Herring & Co., which was bought of you October 16, was burned at the great fire which occurred here on the morning of the 8th instant ; and that the safe underwent and resisted the most intense heat, and was not removed until the afternoon of the 12th instant, having remained in the fire one hundred and eight hours, and brought out the contents in a good state of preservation ; and the paper upon which this is written was part of the contents of said safe.

AVERY & EVANS.

BURNING OF THE SYRACUSE MILLS.

SYRACUSE, N. Y., May 19, 1863.

Messrs. D. S. & S. P. Geer, Agents for Herring & Co.:

On the morning of the 14th instant our mills and storehouse (known as the Syracuse Mills) were destroyed. We were fortunate enough to have one of Herring's Patent Champion Safes in our office, which was subjected to such intense heat as to melt the heavy brass plates and portions of the wrought iron bands. On opening the safe we found our papers (our books having been previously removed) entirely uninjured. We have the utmost confidence in the Champion Safe.

Yours, &c.,

BARKER, TOWNSEND & CO.

BURNING OF BASTABLE ARCADE, OCTOBER 6, 1862.

SYRACUSE, October 7, 1862.

Messrs. D. S. & S. P. Geer, Agents for Herring & Co.:

GENTLEMEN—This is to certify that the Herring's Patent Champion Safe, No. 15,888, which was obtained of you September 21, 1857, has just passed through the fire of the Bastable Arcade of this city, containing all my valuable papers, together with one hundred dollars in bills (which you offered to insure for five dollars), and came out all safe and sound; not a single paper is illegible or materially injured.

I consider Herring's Patent Champion Safe is all that you claim for it.

Yours, &c.,

N. C. POWERS, M. D.

ANOTHER IN THE SAME FIRE.

SYRACUSE, October 8, 1862.

Messrs. D. S. & S. P. Geer, Agents for Herring & Co.'s Safes:

GENTLEMEN—We had in our office one of Herring's Patent Safes, at the destruction of the Bastable Arcade by fire, on the 6th instant. It was in that building and passed through all the fire, not being removed until the morning after, when it was found among the ruins in the cellar. On being opened the contents, consisting of books and valuable papers, were found in a good state of preservation and without material injury.

We are satisfied from the test to which our safe was put that Herring & Co.'s Safes are preferable to all others for their quality of resistance to the action of fire.

Yours, &c.,

SEDGWICK, ANDREWS & KENNEDY.

BURNING OF THE EVERSON BLOCK, March 7, 1866.

SYRACUSE, March 9, 1866.

Messrs. D. S. & S. P. Geer, Agents for Herring & Co.'s Safes:

GENTLEMEN—On the morning of the 7th instant the Everson block, together with my entire stock of goods, was destroyed by fire. I was fortunately the owner of one of Herring's Champion Fire-proof Safes, in which were my accounts and valuable papers. I have just opened it and find them entirely safe and uninjured.

X. SPANG.

ANOTHER IN SAME FIRE.

SYRACUSE, March 9, 1866.

Messrs. D. S. & S. P. Geer, Agents for Herring & Co.:

GENTLEMEN—On the morning of the 7th instant the Everson block was consumed by fire. I was an owner of a flour and feed-store and had a store in said block, and,

Plate No. 12.

No. 5—Folding Door.

56 in. high,
14 in. wide, } Inside.
18 in. deep,

very fortunately for me. I had one of Herring's Safes, which contained all my books and valuable papers. I was very anxious about them (it being a very hot fire), but I am happy to inform you that, on opening the safe, the contents were found uninjured.

SILAS J. CHESEBROUGH.

GREAT FIRE AT TROY, 1854.

TROY, Tuesday, September 5, 1854.

S. C. Herring:

SIR—One of your safes preserved my papers and restored them to me in good order, having been exposed to an intense heat at the late great fire in this city on the 25th ult. Please to forward me one of your improved Herring's Patent Safes, same size as old one, as soon as convenient. I have delivered the old one to your agents in this city, Messrs. Heartt & Co.

Yours truly,
C. W. THOMPSON.

DESTRUCTIVE FIRE IN TROY, 1857.

TROY, August 10, 1857.

Silas C. Herring:

DEAR SIR—I beg leave to return you one of your celebrated fire-proof safes, a little the worse for service, though in a tolerable state of preservation. It passed through the destructive fire which visited us here at an early hour this morning, and was recovered from the ruins not until about everything entering into the composition of the store of a combustible material had been entirely consumed. It contained all my books and more valuable papers than many possess or often risk in safes. The only injury resulting to the books was to be found in the dissolution of the binding; ordinary leather covers to pass-books were found completely melted away and gone, while not a paper was destroyed or rendered illegible. Many of my checks and bills receivable, were used at the bank on the succeeding and other days, leaving evidences of tremendous exposure, as banks here can attest; though not one was so far mutilated as to render it necessary to procure a duplicate or a substitute. I am absolutely the loser of nothing by your safe, save the safe itself (which, I am told, is now rendered unsafe), if I except my books, the binding of which is destroyed and that only; the latter I will brook if you will be kind enough to forward me another safe.

ROYAL BALL.

ANOTHER IN SAME FIRE.

TROY, August 10, 1857.

S. C. Herring & Co.:

I was unfortunate enough, in one respect at least, to be burnt out here this morning and have lost everything except a couple of account books, which happened to be in a safe of your manufacture. Those were entirely uninjured, if I except only the binding. The safe was got out of the ruins by my assistance, not until it had fallen through the cellar and the store wholly consumed. It so happened that the key had been left in the door, and, notwithstanding the intense exposure the safe had gone through, the lock was found to work as freely as at any time previous. The safe yielded up its contents in a perfect state of preservation.

EDWIN BOWMAN.

THE GREAT FIRE IN TROY, MAY 10, 1862.

TWO SAFES IN ONE OFFICE.

RENSSELAER AND SARATOGA RAILROAD OFFICE,
TROY, N. Y., May 14, 1862.

Messrs. Herring & Co., New York :

The folding-door safe of your make which we purchased from you a few years ago for the Rensselaer and Saratoga Railroad Co. was in their office here (in the Union depot) in the great fire on the 10th inst. It was exposed to the general fire of the building and did its duty handsomely. Our books, papers, and seven hundred dollars in money were all preserved ; nothing injured but the binding of the books. The smaller safe which I bought from you was in the same fire and came out with like result. Everything was preserved in a legible condition.

L. H. TUPPER, *Superintendent.*
A. C. LOCKWOOD, *Treasurer.*

TWO MORE IN SAME FIRE.

TROY AND BOSTON RAILROAD OFFICE,
TROY, May 21, 1865.

Messrs Herring & Co., New York :

GENTLEMEN--In reply to your inquiries I would say that we had two safes of your manufacture in our office, at the Union Depot, during the great fire of 10th instant. The contents of both are safe and legible. The safes were broken in opening them, and I now think we will send them both to you for repairs. The small one has preserved its contents quite equal to the large one.

Respectfully yours,
J. V. BAKER,
Superintendent.

AND ANOTHER.

TROY, N. Y., Aug. 9, 1862.

Messrs. Herring & Co., New York :

GENTLEMEN--The iron safe of your make, which was purchased some years ago, was in the center of the Union House—a large, substantial, five-story brick building —when it was entirely destroyed at the great fire in this city, on the 10th of May last. You will remember that several hundred buildings, and over three million dollars' worth of property were lost by this fire. My building was in the midst of the conflagration, and not a drop of water reached the building or safe during the whole of the fire. We dug it out some *two months* after the fire, and found, to my great astonishment, the interior in good condition, and the papers and books which it contained were all preserved, the papers being as good as before the fire.

E. D. BEACH.

FIRE IN BROOKLYN, N. Y., OCTOBER, 1851.

BROOKLYN, October 14, 1851.

Mr. S. C. Herring :

SIR—In the midst of my losses, by the destruction of my manufactory, a few days since, I have the satisfaction to know that all my valuable books and papers and a large amount of gold pens, intrusted to one of your safes for safe-keeping, were preserved uninjured.

The safe stood on the second story and was surrounded by flames until the floor gave way, and then remained in the burning ruins until the next day. When taken out, the brass knob on the door and the name-plate were completely melted

off, and the safe had the appearance of being nearly destroyed; and my surprise, on opening the door, was unbounded to find the contents of the safe in as complete preservation as when put in.

Yours,
JAMES D. STEWART,
Jeweler and Gold Pen Manufacturer.

GREAT FIRE IN BROOKLYN, 1855.

HECKER'S MILLS DESTROYED BY FIRE, AND HERRING'S PATENT CHAMPION SAFES AGAIN TRIUMPHANT!

NEW YORK, October 13, 1855.

Messrs. Herring & Co.:

GENTLEMEN—We take pleasure in stating that the "Herring's Patent Safe," which we purchased from you about a year since, has been the means of preserving our books, papers, &c., from the fire at the destruction of our flour mills, in Brooklyn, early on the morning of the 11th instant. The safe was exposed to a severe heat about eight hours, and when cooled off and opened the contents were found entirely uninjured. We cheerfully recommend your safe to public confidence.

HECKER & BROTHER.

GREAT FIRE AT BINGHAMTON.

BINGHAMTON, N. Y., January 28, 1863.

Messrs. Herring & Co.:

On the 23d day of August last my store and contents were consumed by fire. I was provided with two of your Patent Safes, which contained all my books and papers, and one hundred and eighty dollars in bank-bills, which I am happy to say were preserved to my entire satisfaction. As soon as I get my new store built, I shall want another of your safes.

BENJAMIN F. SISSON.

ANOTHER.

BINGHAMTON, N. Y., January 27, 1863.

Messrs. S. C. Herring & Co.:

GENTLEMEN—On Friday morning, the 23d instant, "Odd Fellows' Hall," in which our store was situated, was consumed by fire. In our store was one of your Patent Safes, which contained all our most valuable goods, books, and papers. Upon opening the safe in the afternoon we were pleased to find everything in perfect order, as much so as when put in the previous evening.

Yours truly,
EVANS & ALLEN,
Watchmakers and Jewelers.

YET ANOTHER.

BINGHAMTON, N. Y., May 7, 1863.

Messrs. Herring & Co.:

GENTLEMEN—At the time of the recent disastrous fire which occurred here January 22, I was among the sufferers. Being in the watch and jewelry business I was obliged to have a safe, which was fortunately one of your manufacture, and proved itself fire-proof by saving my books, papers and goods. I take pleasure in adding this to the numerous testimonials of the security of your excellent safe against fire.

Respectfully yours,
O. N. SWIFT.

THE GREAT FIRE AT POUGHKEEPSIE.

POUGHKEEPSIE, July 25, 1860.

Messrs. Herring & Co. :

GENTLEMEN—On the night of the 23d instant a fire occurred here which extended to sixteen buildings and over. In our furniture building was one of your Patent Champion Safes, which stood before the fire, on the store floor, in such a position as to make it impossible to remove it. Consequently it remained until the floor fell, and then the safe fell into the cellar among a lot of maple and other furniture and combustible materials, where it remained from three o'clock A. M. until ten o'clock. When removed from the ruins every book and paper was found in perfect order. It has saved us many a valuable paper, and our books, which would have been a very serious matter to have lost. The building was a two-story frame building, and cellar ten feet.

ANDRUS & DUDLEY.

BURNING OF THE EAGLE OFFICE.

POUGHKEEPSIE, November, 25, 1862.

Messrs. Herring & Co. :

GENTLEMEN—On the night of the 22d instant a fire occurred in our printing establishment (a four story brick building), which was completely destroyed. The building was filled with papers and printers' ink and burned most furiously and with intense heat. Your safe was in the fire for about ten hours, and when we were able to get at it, and on breaking it open we found our books and papers in perfect order, the covers being only a little warped. With a little repair we consider the safe good for another fire.

Yours, &c.,
PLATT & SCHRAM,
Per J. E. SCHRAM.

FIRE IN RHINEBECK.

STATE DOCK, RHINEBECK, June 16, 1856.

Messrs. S. C. Herring & Co. :

GENTLEMEN—In the fire which destroyed our storehouse on the morning of the 22d of April, 1856, one of your safes, containing our books and papers, was taken from the ruins while it was red hot; after carefully cooling it, we opened it and found our books and papers in good order, the binding only being injured. We have this day ordered a new safe through your Agent, Mr. Green.

Yours respectfully,
JOHN M. KEESE & CO.

GREAT FIRE IN RHINEBECK, MAY 8, 1864.

RHINEBECK, N. Y., May 25, 1864.

Messrs. Herring & Co. :

GENTLEMEN—On the morning of May 8 our village was visited by a very destructive fire, which destroyed several buildings, among them the one I occupied as a jewelry store, which was entirely consumed. I had my books, papers, bonds, and jewelry locked up in one of your Patent Champion Safes, which was subjected to an intense heat. I had it cut open the same day. The contents were all preserved. Every line of my books and papers is perfectly legible The only injury was the discoloration of some of the jewelry by the varnish on the book-case. I am very much pleased with the test of your Champion Safes, and when I rebuild will want another.

Respectfully yours,
WM. J. STYLES.

ANOTHER IN SAME FIRE.

RHINEBECK, N. Y., May 25, 1865.

Messrs. Herring & Co., New York :

GENTLEMEN—The large fire which occurred here on the morning of May 8 totally destroyed the building in which I had my store. Fortunately I had one of your Patent Champion Safes in use, containing my books, papers, money, and some Five-twenty Bonds, which were entirely preserved, although the safe was subjected to a severe test from the burning of pork, hams, and other combustible goods in its immediate vicinity. It stood a good roasting, and every business man should have one for his valuables. The covers of the books were curled up by the steam from the fire-proof composition, which is the only injury the contents sustained, which, as I am informed, is usually the case. I shall want another safe as soon as I again commence business and want none but your Champion.

GEORGE E. RING.

THE GREAT FIRE AT BATH—BURNING OF THE MERCHANTS' EXCHANGE, COUNTY OFFICES, &c.

STEUBEN CO. TREASURER'S OFFICE,
BATH, N. Y., May 6, 1856.

S. C. Herring & Co. :

GENTLEMEN—On the 28th March last, the Merchants' Exchange, a three-story brick block, containing four stores, was destroyed by fire. My office was on the second floor, in which I had one of your safes, which I bought of you in 1852; the safe is No.   , and weighed sixteen hundred pounds. It was exposed to a severe fire and fell to the bottom of the cellar, and remained buried in the hot bricks thirty-six hours. When it was taken out and sufficiently cooled it was unlocked, and the books, papers and money, were all preserved; there is not a line or word but can be read, I am satisfied. The safe has answered my greatest expectations. The locks all work well. The safe has sprung some, but not very badly. Please inform me how much my old safe is worth, or what you would allow me in exchange for a new safe. I want a good one.

Respectfully yours,

P. S. DONAHE,
County Treas.

ANOTHER IN SAME FIRE.

BATH, March 28, 1856.

S. C. Herring & Co. :

GENTLEMEN—I have had this morning an opportunity of testing a safe of your make in the great fire which destroyed the Merchants' Exchange building; although exposed to such intense heat that a portion of the feet and knobs were melted, my books and papers, with the exception of being slightly stained by steam, were preserved in perfectly good condition; and when its place is supplied it shall be with one of Herring's Fire-proof.

Yours respectfully,

HORACE G. DONAHE.

ANOTHER GREAT FIRE AT BATH, NOVEMBER 4, 1859.

BATH, N. Y., November 15, 1859.

Messrs. Herring & Co.:

GENTLEMEN—You have no doubt heard of the great fire which occurred here on the 4th instant, destroying about thirty buildings. My building was consumed with the others, but, fortunately for me, I had, at the time, one of Herring's Safes in use, which was exposed to the heat about twelve hours. The safe contained all my books, papers, one hundred gold and silver watches, and a quantity of jewelry. The books and papers, when taken out of the safe, I found every word and figure as perfect as before the fire ; the watches and jewelry only slightly steamed. This test, with the two safes which you had tested by fire here a few years since, has gained them a great reputation here as a fire-proof safe, and the merchants don't want any other kind.

Yours respectfully,

JOHN S. FARR.

FIRE IN UTICA.

UTICA, January 18, 1856.

S. C. Herring & Co. :

GENTLEMEN—We have a safe of your manufacture that passed through the late fire in this city. We wish to know if it can be refilled and made secure against fire? It is whole and in perfect shape. Please inform us, if it can, what the expense will be. The books and papers contained in the safe came out uninjured.

Yours truly,

WESTCOTT & HAMMOND.

ANOTHER FIRE AT UTICA.

UTICA, N. Y., December 29, 1858.

S. C. Herring & Co. :

GENTLEMEN—At the time of the destruction of the store of J. W. Fuller & Co. by fire, in March last, they had a safe of your manufacture in the building ; since when we have purchased the safe. Although exposed to a severe fire, melting off the name-plates, &c., the books and papers were preserved in good condition.

Yours truly,

J. GRIFFITHS & CO.

THE GREAT FIRE AT JAMESTOWN, JANUARY 20, 1861.

JAMESTOWN BANK.
JAMESTOWN, N. Y., February 6, 1861.

Messrs. Herring & Co., New York :

GENTLEMEN—In reply to your inquiries about the safe of your make which I bought from you for the Jamestown Bank, we would say the safe has resisted the fire well and has answered all our expectations. The fire in which the safe was tried was fully as severe as any that could occur in this place. Over forty-two places of business were destroyed, and our banking-house was in the center of them. We removed many of our books before the fire reached us, but about three thousand dollars in specie, some of our books, and many valuable papers, bonds, mortgages, &c., remained in the safe and passed through the fire. We consider it had a very severe trial, as it fell upon a pile of wood in our cellar. The safe remained in the fire for fourteen hours before we could get it out, the fire still burning under it when removed. Not a drop of water was thrown on the building from the commencement, as the heat was too great for the firemen to get within reach. The safe has done all that you promised. We found our books, money, papers, bonds, mortgages, &c , all safe—no sign of fire and in no way damaged, except being a little steamed.

Yours truly,

ALONZO KENT, *President.*
J. MAYHEW, *Cashier.*

Plate No. 14.

No. 6—With Banker's Chest.

26 in. high, }
17 in. wide, } Inside.
14 in. deep, }

Banker's Chest.
11 in. high, }
17 in. wide, } Outside.
11 in. deep, }

No. 7—High, with Banker's Chest.

28 in. high, }
19 in. wide, } Inside.
15 in. deep, }

Banker's Chest.
11 in. high, }
19 in. wide, } Outside.
15 in. deep, }

ANOTHER SAFE IN THE SAME FIRE.

JAMESTOWN, February 6, 1861.

Messrs. Herring & Co.:

GENTLEMEN— At the great fire which occurred here on the night of the 30th ultimo, the Herring's Patent Champion Safe, which I purchased from you last summer, containing all my books, papers, and money, and a large amount of jewelry, was in my store, which was located in the center of the burning buildings. The fire broke out about half-past eleven o'clock, and, in less than one hour, nearly fifty buildings were in flames, and the whole business portion of the town was threatened with destruction. The heat was so great that, when the fire was raging on both sides of the street, which is an unusually wide one, no person could approach the burning buildings or pass through the street; consequently, not a drop of water was thrown either upon my building, which was the middle of a three story brick block, or upon my safe during the fire. The flames burned fearfully for a long time. The safe fell into the cellar, and was exposed until the fire had exhausted itself. We got it out of the ruins about ten o'clock the next morning, and, finding it would not unlock, were obliged to cut it open. My books, papers, and money were all preserved, no injury being done, except to the binding of the books. A portion of the jewelry was damaged, owing to the steam generated in the safe, which stained and discolored them. The greater part, however, was well preserved, and several watches which were running before the fire were *still running when taken out* of the safe, marking the true time of the day. I return you the old safe to exhibit to your customers (you will see the knobs and plates are all melted off), and wish you to send me another of the same size and kind. I had a safe in my store of Pittsburg manufacture standing near the door, which did not result so well, the inside, with its contents, being entirely (or nearly so) destroyed by the heat.

LEVANT L. MASON.

GREAT FIRE AT OLEAN, AUGUST 7, 1862.

OLEAN, N. Y., August 13, 1862.

Messrs. Herring & Co.:

GENTLEMEN— In the recent destructive fire which occurred here on the morning of August 7th I had one of your fire-proof safes in use, which contained books, papers, &c., which were all preserved without a mark of fire. The combustible material, together with the building, made the fire a very hot one. Still, if my books and papers were to be examined by a stranger, so well have they been preserved, that he would not suppose they had been through such a severe ordeal.

Yours respectfully,

A. ADAMS.

ANOTHER GREAT FIRE IN OLEAN.

THE SAME SAFE AGAIN TESTED.

OLEAN, N. Y., January 20, 1866.

Messrs. Herring & Co.:

GENTLEMEN— I had one of Herring's Double-door Fire-proof Safes, which went through the fire in our village on the 16th of January, 1866. On removing the safe, after being in the fire thirty hours, I opened it and found the papers, &c., just as good as when put in. The wood-work was perfect, not even the varnish being touched. I shall have the safe fixed up and try it again; as this safe went through a fire before preserving all the contents entire. I would sooner try it again than any other make and consider it the best fire-proof safe ever made.

A. ADAMS.

GREAT FIRE AT PLATTSBURGH, N. Y.

In the great fire which completely swept the business portion of this place, some seven "Herring's Safes," on sale in the store of Messrs. Fitch & Cook, of that place, were enveloped in the burning mass; and, although not removed until the fire had completely exhausted itself, yet the interior wood-work and contents of every safe was untouched with even a mark of fire. One or two of the above contained books and papers. All were restored in perfect order.

FIRE AT DEPOSIT, N. Y., MARCH 14, 1851.

DEPOSIT, April 26, 1851.

Mr. S. C. Herring:

DEAR SIR—Duty demands that I should add my testimony among the thousand others that have witnessed the efficacy of your well-established Fire-proof Safes. My store was discovered to be on fire about one o'clock in the morning of the 14th of March last, which destroyed everything in the store except the safe and its contents. The store was built of very heavy timber, with double floors above and below, which caused the fire to burn upon the inside several hours before it was discovered. When I reached the place the fire was breaking out on both sides of the store, which soon brought the safe in sight, which was as hot as fire could make it, being in the hottest part of the fire; it remained there four hours after it was discovered. Other buildings being out of danger, the attention of our citizens was now called to the safe, which was still surrounded by a bed of coals and white with heat. We extracted the safe as soon as possible, and after cooling it sufficiently, I unlocked it and found, to my great surprise, my books and papers in good and legible order.

Truly yours,

A. M. CABLE.

DESTRUCTIVE FIRE AT PORT JERVIS.

PORT JERVIS, N. Y., June 15, 1866.

Silas C. Herring, Esq.:

DEAR SIR—On Tuesday night, the 12th instant, our store was burned to the ground, together with the entire stock of goods. Our books, papers, &c., were in one of your Fire-proof Safes. After being in a very hot fire, so hot that we could not get it out for ten hours, we found the books, moneys, papers, &c., all right—just as good as new, except some of the leather bindings. Our object in writing to you is to learn what it can be fixed up for, or how you will exchange it for a new one of the same size. By giving this your earliest attention you will greatly oblige,

Yours respectfully,

A. VAN ETTEN & SON.

GREAT FIRE AT OGDENSBURGH.

We, the undersigned, having been present at the opening of one of Silas C. Herring's Safes, in the store of Messrs. Watrous & Lawrence, after the great fire on the 19th October, are free to acknowledge this as the greatest triumph we ever witnessed of a Salamander Safe. The fire in the stores of Messrs Watrous & Lawrence and H. S. Humphrey & Co. was much hotter than in any other part of the burnt district—its intensity being increased by the large quantity of oil, camphene, alcohol, and other combustible matter in the drug-store. One of the feet of the safe was entirely burnt off, and a quantity of iron and nails were melted together in one solid mass, so great was the heat. Yet, notwithstanding all this, every paper was preserved entire and the writing perfectly legible, the varnish having been untouched.

(Signed,) J. C. BARTER, *Collector of the Port of Ogdensburgh.*
GEORGE ROBINSON, *Postmaster of Ogdensburgh.*
I. HASBROUCK, *Agent of Etna Insurance Company of Hartford.*
EDWIN M. HOLBROOK.
B. H. VARY, *Agent for American Insurance Co.*
W. J. PARDEE, *General Agent of Etna of Hartford Insurance Co.*
SAMUEL H. PRICE, *General Agent of Northwestern Insurance Co.*
D. M. CHAPIN, *Agent of Springfield and Marine and Protection of Hartford Ins. Cos.*

GREAT FIRE AT OSWEGO, N. Y.

The only safe in the great fire at Oswego that was exposed to the intense heat, which preserved the books, papers, and money uninjured.

OSWEGO, July 10, 1853.

Silas C. Herring, Esq., New York :

SIR—The Patent Safe which we purchased from you some six years since, was severely tested by the great fire which occurred here on the 5th instant. Our warehouse, in which the safe was located, was a large wooden building, and filled at the time with a large quantity of merchandise, among which were considerable turpentine, alcohol, &c., making an unusually hot fire. A large quantity of kegs of nails in the vicinity of the safe was melted into solid masses. The brass knob and brass plates on the safe were melted off and the iron very much warped ; yet we have the pleasure to announce to you that our books, valuable papers, and about two thousand dollars in bank-bills, were all saved uninjured. The safe was not removed until the building and contents were entirely burned, the safe having undergone the most severe test as to its capacity to resist heat. We would like you to ship us another, of larger size and equal quality as soon as possible, for, in our opinion, no prudent business man should be without one of your genuine safes. The loss of our books and papers could not be repaired, and we are indebted to your safe for their preservation.

Yours,
FITZHUGH & LITTLEJOHN.

FIRE IN GREENPORT, L. I.

GREENPORT, L. I., September 6, 1854.

S. C. Herring :

SIR—On the 31st of August a destructive fire occurred on our premises, which destroyed our store and contents, with the exception of our books, money ($1,500), and valuable papers, which were preserved in one of your truly valuable safes. We cheerfully recommend to all having valuables to preserve from fire to inclose them in one of your safes. We shall require two in future, and will use no other.

WELLS & CARPENTER.

FIRE AT LEROY, N. Y.

LE ROY, March 1, 1855.

Mr. S. C. Herring :

SIR—I deem it an act of justice to inform you that I was the owner of one of your Champion Safes, in which were my books and papers when my store was destroyed by fire on the 13th of January last ; and although the safe was exposed to an intense heat for about six hours, and during the time covered with burning timbers, I am pleased to say that all my books and papers were restored uninjured.

Yours,
J. M. FOREMAN.

FIRE AT FISHKILL PLAINS, N. Y.

FISHKILL PLAINS, December 1, 1857.

S. C. Herring & Co. :

GENTLEMEN— One of your safes was in my father's flouring mill some time since, when it was destroyed by fire, and your safe preserved the books and papers entire; and since then we have had the greatest confidence in your safes.

R. S. VAN WYCK.

FIRE AT ORISKANY FALLS, N. Y.

ORISKANY FALLS, January 4, 1858.

S. C. Herring & Co. :

GENTLEMEN—The Herring's Safe I purchased from you some time since was subjected to a severe test of fire on the morning of the 31st day of December, being enveloped in flames made of turpentine, oil, &c. My store and its contents were completely destroyed, with the exception of what was intrusted in the safe. My books, bonds, money, notes, and insurance policies were saved, and I think your safe deserves the name of Champion. I will forward you the safe and will require another the same size.

D. S. BUCKINGHAM.

FIRE AT SING SING, N. Y.

SING SING, N. Y., November 28, 1859.

Herring & Co. :

DEAR SIRS—I this day forward to your address my old safe, per propeller Ora. This safe was in the large fire at Sing Sing prison on the 2d day of October last, and was subjected to an intense heat, and remained in the ruins eight hours after the fire was subdued. Not having the key at hand, I was necessarily compelled to break the door open, and, to my great astonishment, I found my books preserved without a single leaf being burnt. I will thank you to send me another of the same size per return propeller.

Respectfully yours,

BENJ. UNDERWOOD.

FIRE AT MEDINA, N. Y.

MEDINA, N. Y., December 23, 1859.

S. C. Herring & Co. :

GENTLEMEN— On the morning of the 18th instant, our establishment at this place, known as the Orleans Mills, with two extension warehouses attached, was destroyed by fire. The combustible materials lending rapidity to the flames prevented our saving anything in the buildings, with the exception of our books and papers, which we were fortunate enough to have in one of your safes. After sixteen hours of intense heat the safe was taken out red hot, and surrendered its contents without the least appearance of having undergone such a test. For further proof of this we refer you to the citizens of this place who saw it opened and expressed their satisfaction at the result.

HILL, WHALEN & CO.

Plate No. 15.

No. 8—High, with Banker's Chest.

32 in. high, }
22 in. wide, } Inside.
15 in. deep, }

Banker's Chest.
14 in. high, }
22 in. wide, } Outside.
15 in. deep, }

No. 1/2—Folding Door, with Banker's Chest.

34 in. high, }
24 in. wide, } Inside.
16 in. deep, }

Banker's Chest.
14 in. high, }
24 in. wide, } Outside.
15 in. deep, }

FIRE AT OWEGO, N. Y.

Owego, N. Y., March 23, 1860.

S. C. Herring & Co. :

Gentlemen—The safe we purchased from you a short time since preserved our books and papers of great value to us safely during the great fire of the 20th instant. It was opened as soon as we could get it out of the ruins, being sixteen hours, and unlocked as perfectly as it ever had done. Will it be safe to risk it again?

Yours,

STONE & CO.

GREAT FIRE AT WHITEHALL, N. Y.

Whitehall, N. Y., April 17, 1860.

Messrs. Herring & Co. :

Gentlemen—On the 13th of April, 1860, a large fire occurred here, destroying several stores, including one of the banks.

In my drug-store was one of your safes, which stood an intense heat for several hours, among oils, turpentine, and other combustible matter, such as is used in every drug-store. The glass ware was all melted into one mass. Every one said and expected the contents of said safe, including books and papers, would be totally destroyed; and even my faith was shaken when I saw the test it was subjected to. I opened the safe in the presence of the President of Whitehall Bank, and others, and, to my utmost astonishment and surprise, every article was preserved, the papers all in as good condition as when put in. I have ordered, through your agent, another one.

E. W. HALL.

FIRE ON THE HUDSON RIVER.

Coeymans, Albany County, N. Y., August 1, 1860.

Messrs. Herring & Co. :

Gentlemen—We were so fortunate as to have our books, papers, silver, and a large amount of money in bank bills in the safe we bought from you two years ago, on board the propeller T. C. Durant, on Friday last, July 27. When that steamer caught fire and was burned, the safe was on deck in the captain's office, and exposed to an intense heat; in fact, some gold in the money-drawer several feet from the safe was melted, while the entire contents of the safe were preserved with hardly the smell of fire. There was a canister of powder in the safe, besides our money and valuables; yet everything was saved, even to the powder.

SCHOONMAKER & JOHNSON.

FIRE AT DUNDEE, N. Y.

Dundee, N. Y., December 5, 1860.

Messrs. Herring & Co. :

Gentlemen—The safe in the fire on the 27th ultimo was the same one you sold me two years ago. It was a $60 size, and is now owned by Fred Smith, a jeweler. It was in a three-story brick building in the hottest part of the fire; was in the fire twelve hours. When they got it out he was very much excited, and poured water on it. When cooled off, it was opened by a blacksmith; as the safe and lock-work were so much heated, it could not be unlocked with the key. He found his jewelry all safe—watches all ticking, bank-bills all right. I have a five-dollar bill in my pocket that was in the safe at the time. The brass knob on the door was melted off. Some of the jewelry slightly damaged by steam; but this, I think, was caused by the water thrown on the safe to cool it.

Yours truly,

D. E. BEDELL.

FIRE AT STATEN ISLAND.

January 23, 1861.

Messrs. Herring & Co. :

GENTLEMEN— A large fire occurred here on the 22d of October last, which destroyed our workshop. In our office we had one of your safes, which preserved our books and papers, amounting in value to $20,000. The safe was surrounded by lumber, which made a tremendous heat. We do not consider our valuables secure without one of your safes.

Respectfully yours,
ROBINSON & MULFORD.

FIRE IN DUNKIRK, N. Y.

DUNKIRK, N. Y., April 26, 1861.

Messrs. Herring & Co. :

GENTLEMEN—At the large fire which occurred here, October 19, 1856, our store was destroyed. We had our books, valuable papers, &c., saved from destruction through the security of your Fire-proof Safe. The fire was extremely hot ; besides the building and other combustible materials, we had some oil, turpentine, and varnish on hand, which gave the safe a pretty severe roasting. We are very much pleased with this test, and take pleasure in recommending your safes to the public.

Respectfully yours,
T. R. COLEMAN & CO.

FIRE AT CARTHAGE, N. Y.

CARTHAGE, N. Y., July 17, 1861.

Messrs. Herring & Co. :

GENTLEMEN — In the large fire which occurred in our place on Sunday night last, my store was destroyed. One of your Patent Champion Safes, which I bought from you last fall, was removed from the building to the street, though it is doubtful if this change did not expose it to a hotter fire than if it had been left untouched. The fire swept both sides of the street, and the wind kept the flames constantly on the safe. After the fire I found the contents well preserved. Everything in the safe was perfect, except that the leather binding of the books was affected by the steam.

Respectfully yours,
C. N. BOW.

FIRE AT UNION SPRINGS, N. Y.

UNION SPRINGS, N. Y., December 19, 1861.

Messrs. Herring & Co. :

GENTLEMEN- On the morning of the 30th of November last a large fire occurred in this place, consuming some five or six stores ; and among the number was ours, with all its contents.

We were fortunate in being provided with one of your safes, which contained all our books, papers, &c., which, we are happy to inform you, were preserved uninjured, after being exposed to a severe test.

Respectfully yours,
CURRY & HATHORN.

THE GREAT FIRE AT COOPERSTOWN, N. Y.

COOPERSTOWN, N. Y., April 18, 1862.

Messrs. Herring & Co., New York:

GENTLEMEN—The safe of your make, purchased from your store some time ago—size No. 1, low folding-door—passed through the great fire here, being subjected to a heat of *ten hours* of an intense character. My books had been removed, but all the papers left in the safe were taken out afterward in perfect order, only discolored by steam. The safe has proved itself perfectly fire-proof. Yours, &c.,

JOHN F. SCOTT.

FIRE IN BURDETT, SCHUYLER COUNTY, N. Y.

BURDETT, N. Y., August 30, 1862.

Messrs. Herring & Co.:

It affords me pleasure to say that when my store was destroyed by fire on the 15th ultimo I was so fortunate as to have one of your Champion Safes, in which were my books, papers, money, some plate and jewelry, all of which were preserved entire, without any injury.

The safe was exposed to an intense heat for thirteen hours, surrounded by coal-oil, and other very combustible materials. I shall want another safe soon, and shall have none but yours.

G. R. BURDETT,

per MYRON RAPLEE.

FIRE IN WELLSVILLE, N. Y.

WELLSVILLE, N. Y., May 4, 1863.

Messrs. Herring & Co.:

GENTLEMEN—My store was entirely destroyed by the fire which occurred here on the night of April 28.

I had one of your Patent Champion Safes in use, and although it had a severe roasting, it was the means of preserving my books and papers. I shall order a new one of you as soon as I have use for it.

Respectfully yours,

E. P. CLARK.

GREAT FIRE IN GLENS FALLS, N. Y.

GLENS FALLS, N. Y., June 4, 1864.

Messrs. Herring & Co.:

GENTLEMEN—My store was entirely destroyed by fire at the very destructive conflagration which left the business portion of this village in ashes on the 31st of May last.

I had in use one of your make of safes which was purchased some years ago, and which preserved its contents to my entire satisfaction. I cheerfully recommend your safes to all who are in want of a good fire-proof safe.

Yours, &c.,

WM. CRONKHITE.

FIRE IN BREWERTON, N. Y.

BREWERTON, N. Y., August 7, 1864.

Messrs. Herring & Co.:

GENTLEMEN—On the 30th day of November, 1857, I purchased of your agents, D. S. and S. P. Geer, at Syracuse, one of your Champion Safes, No. 16,212, which was burned, together with my store, on the morning of the 5th day of August, 1864. It contained my books, papers, and other valuables; and I am happy to state to you that, after resisting great heat (the brass plate and knob being melted), it brought out its contents in a good state of preservation. And I would also say that I have the utmost confidence in your Champion Safes, and would recommend all business men to purchase one, as no man should be without one.

D. H. WATERBURY.

FIRE IN RUSHFORD, N. Y.

RUSHFORD, N. Y., January 24, 1865.

Messrs. Herring & Co.:

GENTLEMEN—The safe of your manufacture which I bought from you a few years since has been severely tested and done its duty well. On the 17th of March last my store, with its contents, was entirely destroyed by fire. Your safe contained all my books, valuable papers, and over three thousand dollars in money, and you may well imagine the interest with which I awaited the issue. It was in the hottest of the fire, and I cannot think a safe ever likely to be exposed to a more trying ordeal than this was. Everything it contained was well preserved; nothing injured by fire; even the bank-bills were as good money as when they were first put in the safe.

JOHN H. TOUSLEY.

THE GREAT FIRE IN MEXICO, N. Y.

MEXICO, OSWEGO Co., N. Y., July 20, 1864.

Messrs. Herring & Co., 251 Broadway, New York:

GENTLEMEN—At the time of the late disastrous fire at this place, the Herring Safe belonging to the county of Oswego and occupied by the Surrogate contained all my valuable papers, placed there for safe-keeping. I had therein $2,500 of five-twenty bonds, about $500 in currency, together with mortgages, notes, will, inventory, and vouchers of the estate of the late O. H. Whitney, representing and accounting for value equal to $50,000. All these passed through the fire in perfect safety. The greenbacks are yet legal tender, and the papers are hardly discolored; envelopes and postage stamps are yet fit for use, and the five-twenty bonds are in as perfect condition as when they passed the hands of the printer. The safe was in the second story, fell to the cellar, and there lay till it could be removed, preserving its contents as above stated through the hottest fire ever known in our unfortunate village.

Respectfully yours,

D. W. C. PECK.

FIRE AT MOTTVILLE, N. Y.

MOTTVILLE, N. Y., December 26, 1865.

Messrs. Herring & Co., New York:

GENTLEMEN—We have one of your safes that has been through a fire. Our store was burned on the 15th of October last. The safe fell into the cellar and was red-

Plate No. 16.

No. 1—High, Folding Door, with Banker's Chest.

38 in. high,
24 in. wide, } Inside.
16 in. deep,

Banker's Chest.
14 in. high,
24 in. wide, } Outside.
16 in. deep,

No. 2—High, Folding Door, with Banker's Chest.

41 in. high,
24 in. wide, } Inside.
16 in. deep,

Banker's Chest.
16 in. high,
24 in. wide, } Outside.
16 in. deep,

hot for nearly three hours. The papers and books were well preserved; and though the iron on the outside was burned through, the money, &c., came out all right. Now we wish to know whether you can repair it; also, the price of a new one the same size or a size larger. We have built a new store since and are selling goods again, and do not like to be without our best Insurance Company—the safe.

Respectfully yours,

BENEDICT BROTHERS,
Mottville, Onondaga county, N. Y.

SEVERE FIRE AT YONKERS.

OFFICE OF THE "STATESMAN," YONKERS, March 19, 1866.

Messrs. Herring & Co., New York:

GENTLEMEN—On the night of the 3d of January last the village of Yonkers was visited by a very destructive fire, destroying the whole of the Farrington Building. The office of *The Statesman* was on the second floor, and everything it contained was consumed, with the exception of the contents of one of your Champion Safes (No. 21,975) which, I am happy to say, were preserved in perfect order after being in the burning ruins for nearly one week. I am much pleased to add my testimony to the superiority of your safes, and shall want another.

Very respectfully yours,

M. F. ROWE,
Publisher of THE STATESMAN.

GREAT FIRE AT SARATOGA—BURNING OF CONGRESS HALL.

SARATOGA SPRINGS, N. Y., June 1, 1866.

Messrs. Herring, Farrel & Sherman,
251 Broadway, New York:

GENTLEMEN—You have already learned, through the papers, that Congress Hall in this village, was totally destroyed by fire on the night of Monday, May 28. We had one of your Herring's Patent Champion Safes. Its peculiar location prevented its removal. It remained nearly in the center of the building surrounded on all sides by the flames, and those who witnessed this terrible fire can testify to its terrific heat. We were unable to open the safe until this morning, when we found our insurance policies, with other valuable papers and money, in an excellent state of preservation. This was a severe test of the qualities of your Patent Champion Safe. Nobly did it sustain the standard reputation so well established with the business men of the country. We do not intend to do business in future without one.

Respectfully yours,

H. H. HATHORN & CO.,
Proprietors of Congress Hall.

GREAT FIRE AT BUTTERNUTS—SEPTEMBER, 1866.

BUTTERNUTS, OTSEGO Co., N. Y., September 13, 1866.

Messrs. Herring, Farrel & Sherman:

GENTLEMEN—The great fire that has burned so much of our beautiful and flourishing little village originated at the corner store, spreading in two directions and carrying destruction to all that came in contact with its fiery darts, until seven stores, harness-shop, saloon, cabinet-shop, three dwelling-houses, large dwelling-house and shoe-store, dwelling-house, harness-shop and office, and two dentists' offices, were completely destroyed. The noble little safe I purchased of you stood the test to a charm; it was badly burned and defaced on the outside, but the contents were all safe. This was the only safe in the fire. When got out it was in the building where the fire originated, and I should say in the hottest of the fire. We have no engine in this village to assist at a fire, so the noble little safe had to stand the burn. The test of this convinces me that Herring & Co.'s Safe is *the* safe.

Respectfully, WILLIAM OLIVER.

GREAT FIRE IN BUTTERNUTS.

BUTTERNUTS, N. Y., Oct. 23, 1866.

Messrs. Herring, Farrel & Sherman, New York :

GENTLEMEN—Our village was visited by a serious conflagration on the 17th August last, in which it was my misfortune to be one of the sufferers. The fire commenced about midnight in my store, and was not arrested until fourteen buildings were entirely destroyed. Nothing was to be found in my store after the fire but one of your Patent Safes; the building and stock of goods were a total loss, not a drop of water having been put on. We found the safe in the cellar, and it was red-hot when discovered. It fell near where a barrel of kerosene was kept, which probably helped to "roast" it ; at all events, the brass knob and plates in front of the safe were all melted off, and I had great fears that the fire had been too severe for it. We managed to cool it off after a while, and, when we finally got it open, you may judge of my agreeable surprise to find everything all saved. The covers of the books were somewhat stained, but aside from this everything in the safe was as good for use as if there had been no fire.

Respectfully yours, J. C. TRUMAN.

PHILADELPHIA.

THE GREAT FIRE IN STRAWBERRY STREET.

PHILADELPHIA, March 29, 1852.

Mr. John Farrel, *Agent* :

SIR—It affords us much satisfaction to inform you that the Herring Safe which we purchased of you a short time since preserved our books and papers in good condition during the severe ordeal through which it passed at the disastrous conflagration that took place at our warehouse on the morning of the 28th instant, when the safe was exposed to the most intense heat for some hours, and when dragged from the flames was red-hot on several sides. We make this statement by way of bearing testimony to the worth of these valuable fire-proofs.

Very respectfully, LEWIS & CO.

GREAT FIRE IN CHESTNUT STREET.

BURNING OF WELSH'S CIRCUS, CHINESE MUSEUM, &C., JULY 5, 1854.

PHILADELPHIA, July 7, 1854.

Messrs. Farrel & Co. :

GENTLEMEN—The Herring Fire-proof Safe which we purchased from you, and had in use in our store, 214 Chestnut street, on the night of its destruction by the great fire of the 5th instant, after an exposure of nearly twenty-four hours to intense heat, has proved more than equal to our expectations. It was situated in the very centre of our store, and was the only article, with its contents, that remained in

Plate No. 17.
No. 3—Folding Door, with Banker's Chest.

41 in. high,
32 in. wide, } Inside.
17 in. deep,

Banker's Chest.
20 in. high,
32 in. wide, } Outside.
17 in. deep,

No. 3—Folding Door, with Banker's Chest, half Size.

41 in. high,
32 in. wide, } Inside.
17 in. deep,

Banker's Chest.
20 in. high,
16 in. wide, } Outside.
17 in. deep,

the building which was not entirely destroyed. Everything in the safe was perfectly preserved. We shall want another of your safes, of larger size, as soon as we become located.

     Yours,   THOS. W. EVANS & CO.

ANOTHER.

PHILADELPHIA, July 11, 1854.

Messrs. Farrel & Co.:

GENTLEMEN—At the recent extensive fire in Chestnut street I was located directly in front of the building known as "Welsh's Circus," or National Theater. The Herring Fire proof Safe which I purchased from you about one year since was exposed to a great heat and stood the fire well. I cheerfully bear testimony to the entire preservation of my books, papers, and money in good order, with the exception of being somewhat stained by steam.

     Respectfully yours,
       C. T. AMSLER.
        By J. SYZ, *Attorney*.

THE GREAT FIRE AT FIFTH AND CHESTNUT STREETS, DEC. 14, 1854.

AGAIN HERRING'S SAFE THE CHAMPION!

PHILADELPHIA, December 16th, 1854.

Messrs. Farrel & Co., No. 34 Walnut street:

The Herring's Patent Champion Safe which I bought of you nearly two years since has "turned up" all right. We dug it from the ruins in the cellar yesterday. The safe was in the back part of the fourth story of Fetteral's Buildings, corner of Fifth and Chestnut streets, on the night of the great fire of the 14th inst., and fell with the burning timbers. It contained all my books and papers. My stock, consisting of blank-books and paper, was very large, as I had recently taken in a quantity of paper, which was piled up in stacks near the safe, exposing it to great heat. Not a thing was saved on my premises except the contents of your safe, which effectually resisted all the "fury of the flames." I am now using the same books and papers.

     Yours truly,   THOS. W. PRICE.

BURNING OF THE ARTISAN BUILDING.

PHILADELPHIA, April 12th, 1856.

Messrs. Farrel & Herring:

GENTLEMEN—The Herring's Fire-proof Safe which we purchased from you some time since was in the fourth story of the Artisan Building, on the night of its destruction by fire, April 10th, 1856. The Safe was taken from the ruins yesterday, the exterior showing no injury from the effects of its fearful fall; and when opened our jewelry, which was of great value, was found to be in excellent order. We have no hesitation in recommending your safes to the public as in *every way* worthy of their confidence.

     Yours respectfully,   GEO. W. SIMONS & Co.

GREAT FIRE AT SIXTH AND MARKET STREETS, MAY 1, 1856.

PHILADELPHIA, May 2d, 1856.

Messrs. Farrel & Herring:

GENTLEMEN—The Herring's Patent Champion Fire-proof Safe which we purchased from you in the month of January last was situated in our counting-room, in the second story of No. 231 Market street, on the night of the great fire, 1st of May, 1856, and fell with the burning building in that conflagration. The safe was reached this afternoon, after an exposure of THIRTY-SIX HOURS to intense heat; and although the brass plates on the front of the safe melted, and the exterior shows the evidence of extreme heat, the inside casing was found to be UNTOUCHED BY FIRE, and, with the exception of being a little steamed, is now AS GOOD AS NEW.

EDWARD SEAMANS & CO.

ANOTHER IN THE SAME FIRE.

PHILADELPHIA, May 3d, 1856.

Messrs. Farrel & Herring:

GENTLEMEN- The Herring's Patent Champion Fire-proof Safe of your manufacture which we purchased nearly a year since was in the center of our building at the time of its destruction in the great fire of May 1, 1856.

We had removed the greatest portion of our books before the fire reached us, but left some of them, together with a number of loose papers, inside purposely to test the security of the safe. After thirty-eight hours of severe roasting we found the interior of the safe, upon opening, not only bright and sound, but the books and papers as free from fire as when first put in.

We shall require another safe as soon as we get a new location, and want none but your CHAMPION.

Yours, &c.,
FISHER & BROTHER,
No. 15 North Sixth street.

BURNING OF THE GIRARD BUILDINGS.

PHILADELPHIA, February 3, 1857.

Messrs. Farrel & Herring:

GENTLEMEN—The Herring's Patent Safe which I bought from you a few years ago was in the late fire at the Girard Buildings on the 28th ult., and has given entire satisfaction. The safe was taken from the building and opened this morning; it contained all my books, insurance policies, and valuable papers, which were found to be ALL SAFE.

Yours, &c.,
WILLIAM H. SICKLES,
Printer, late of No. 102 Chestnut street.

DESTRUCTIVE FIRE IN MARKET STREET.

PHILADELPHIA, December, 1857.

Messrs. Farrel & Herring:

GENTLEMEN At the destructive fire in Market street, above Eighth, on the night of the 6th inst., in which our warehouse was entirely consumed, the Herring's Patent Safe of your manufacture which we bought from you some nineteen months ago was in the second story of our building, and contained all our books of accounts, valuable papers, &c. The safe fell with the ruins, and was taken out and opened yesterday; not a paper was scorched, not a line of writing was injured; every article in the safe was preserved in excellent order.

Truly yours,
DAVIS & STEEL.

ANOTHER LARGE FIRE IN CHESTNUT STREET.

PHILADELPHIA, January 19, 1860.

Messrs. Farrel, Herring & Co., 629 Chestnut street:

GENTLEMEN--We have recovered the Herring's Patent Champion safe of your make which we bought from you nearly five years ago, from the ruins of our build-

Plate No. 18.

No. 3½—High, Folding Door, with Banker's Chest.

Banker's Chest.

50 in. high, } Inside.
32 in. wide,
17 in. deep,

20 in. high, } Outside.
32 in. wide,
17 in. deep,

ing, No. 716 Chestnut street, which was entirely destroyed by fire on the morning of the 17th instant.

So rapid was the progress of the flames, before we could reach the store the whole interior was one mass of fire. The safe, being in the back part of the store and surrounded by the most combustible materials, was exposed to great heat. It fell with the walls of that part of the building into the cellar, and remained imbedded in the ruins for more than thirty hours.

The safe was opened this morning in the presence of a number of gentlemen, and the contents, comprising our books, bills receivable, money, and a large amount of valuable papers, are all safe; not a thing was touched by fire.

Respectfully yours, THEO. H. PETERS & CO.

BURNING OF WALLACE'S COAL OIL FACTORY.

PHILADELPHIA, April 7, 1862.

Messrs. Farrel, Herring & Co., No. 629 Chestnut street :

GENTLEMEN- In justice to you and the public, I would state that the Herring's Patent Safe I purchased of you stood the fire. I had it in use at my coal oil factory in Haydock street, which was destroyed by fire on the 31st ult. My books, papers, money—and in fact everything it contained—came out in perfect condition. As soon as I get settled I will call and select another one, having perfect confidence in the superior fire-proof qualities of the Herring Safe.

JOHN K. WALLACE,
Proprietor of Keystone Coal Oil Works.

GREAT FIRE IN CHESTNUT STREET, JANUARY 1, 1866.

PHILADELPHIA, January 2, 1866.

Messrs. Farrel, Herring & Co.:

GENTLEMEN—We have just opened our safe, one of your manufacture, which passed through the destructive fire in Chestnut street last night. The safe was in our office, No. 607, which building was entirely destroyed. The safe was in a warm place, as you may well suppose, and was red-hot when taken out of the embers. We are well satisfied with the result of this trial, and our books, papers, and some $10,000 in money, are almost as perfect as when put in the safe. Nothing is injured, if we except the leather bindings of the books, which are steamed; the money and papers are as good as ever.

Yours truly,
WELLS, FARGO & CO.,
Per J. H. COOK, *Agent.*

DESTRUCTION OF DOLBY'S PLANING-MILLS BY FIRE.

PHILADELPHIA, August 9, 1862.

Messrs. Farrel, Herring & Co., No. 629 Chestnut street :

GENTLEMEN –On Friday, the 8th instant, I was so unfortunate as to have my planing-mills totally destroyed by fire, together with their contents, the machinery being melted by the intensity of the heat; in fact, the only articles saved were contained in one of your invaluable safes, which, although exposed to an intense heat for many hours, to my surprise and gratification, rendered up its contents in a perfect state of preservation. The brass plate on front of the safe was melted.

Please send me one of your No. 2 Folding-door Safes, to use until permanently situated, when I will make arrangements for a larger one.

L. B. M. DOLBY

BURNING OF JONES' PLANING-MILL, TWENTY-FIRST AND CHESTNUT STREETS.

PHILADELPHIA, May 2, 1866.

Messrs. Farrel, Herring & Co. :

GENTLEMEN—My planing-mill and stock on hand were destroyed by fire yesterday morning about six o'clock. The only thing saved was the contents of one of your truly valuable Fire-proof Safes. My building was one hundred and twenty feet long and forty feet wide, and the safe was in the hottest of the fire, and when it was removed, in the afternoon, and opened, my books, papers, &c., were found, to my surprise and gratification, uninjured.

Yours truly,

J. D. JONES.

PENNSYLVANIA.

BURNING OF THE CUMBERLAND VALLEY RAILROAD BUILDINGS AT CHAMBERSBURG.

CHAMBERSBURG, PA., October 22, 1862.

Messrs. Farrel, Herring & Co., Philadelphia :

GENTLEMEN—One of the freaks of the rebels in their recent raid was to burn our depot (Cumberland Valley Railroad Company), in which one of your safes was subjected to a very severe test for four days.

In justice to you we will say that we were present at the opening of the safe and found the contents in an excellent state of preservation.

A. A. LULL, *Superintendent*.
W. B. GILMORE, *Ticket Agent*.
GEORGE A. CEITZ, *A. Q. M.*
J. H. EYSTER.
A. S. HULL.

BURNING OF THE TOWN OF CHAMBERSBURG, JULY 30, 1864.

NUMBER ONE.

CHAMBERSBURG, PA., August 15, 1864.

Messrs. Farrel, Herring & Co. :

GENTLEMEN—On the 30th of last month we had our place of business burned out by the rebels. We had one of your safes in our store at the time ; the safe fell to the cellar, where we had a stock of tar, turpentine, oils, &c. The heat was so intense that we despaired of saving any of the contents. Judge of our surprise on opening it to find our books in good order. A few papers were discolored by steam, but sustained no injury. Please send us another safe soon.

HUBER & TOLBERT.

NUMBER TWO.

CHAMBERSBURG, PA., August 16, 1864.

Messrs. Farrel, Herring & Co.:

GENTLEMEN—I had one of your Fire-proof Safes at the time of the late rebel raid, July 30, when I was burned out. The safe was in my beer-house. It came out all right; it saved my books and papers.

GEORGE LUDWIG.

NUMBER THREE.

CHAMBERSBURG, PA., August 16, 1864.

Messrs. Farrel, Herring & Co.:

GENTLEMEN—At the burning of our town by the rebels, July 30, I had one of your make of safes. It laid in the ruins for six weeks. Judge of my surprise to find my books, papers, and money in perfect order.

SAMUEL F. GREENAWALT.

NUMBER FOUR.

CHAMBERSBURG, PA., August 15, 1864.

Messrs. Farrel, Herring & Co.:

GENTLEMEN—I had in use, at the time of the burning of this place by the rebels (July 30) one of your safes. Owing to the great heat it could not be got at until August 5, when I had the brick so far removed from the cellar (where the safe had fallen) as to enable me to open it. The safe was in such condition that I feared the contents would prove a charred mass, and entail a heavy loss in accounts, &c.

My books were removed so hot that the hand could not remain on them, owing to the steam from contents of cellar and lining of safe. They were permitted to remain in the basket until this day, when, upon a more careful examination, I find them legible and not burnt, as I at first supposed. They, of course, are very much stained from steam, and the bindings destroyed from some cause; but as far as I have examined I can transcribe all the accounts.

Yours respectfully,

J. S. NIXON,

Druggist.

NUMBER FIVE.

CHAMBERSBURG, August 15, 1864.

Messrs. Farrel, Herring & Co.:

GENTLEMEN—I have had in use one of your unequaled safes for a period of four years. My law office was entirely consumed in the fearful conflagration of this place on July 30. The safe fell into the cellar, where it has lain among the ruins until this date. To-day it was removed and found too hot to bear the naked hand. It was necessary to cool it with water before opening it; yet, after having passed through this extraordinary fire and remaining hot for sixteen days, the papers, although discolored by steam, are perfectly legible.

GEORGE W. BREWER.

BURNING OF ODD FELLOWS' HALL.

WRIGHTSVILLE, PA., August 30, 1862.

Messrs. Farrel, Herring & Co.:

GENTLEMEN—On the night of the 28th of this month we had the misfortune to have our Odd Fellows' Hall burned out. We had one of your Champion Safes in it at the time on the third floor; it fell down into the cellar and laid in the fire until the next evening, when it was taken out. On opening it we found everything all safe. We consider it to be the hottest fire we ever had in the place. The brass knob and plate on the door were melted off.

A. BARTON SLOAT,
N. G., of the Chikuaha Lodge No. 317.

THE RAID IN PENNSYLVANIA.
ANOTHER SUFFERER.

WRIGHTSVILLE, PA., July 8, 1863.

Messrs. Farrel, Herring & Co.:

GENTLEMEN—I had one of your Fire-proof Safes at the time of the rebel raid at this place. After the bridge was burned, or at the time, it set fire to the lumber-yard and warehouses. We consider the safe is worthy of the name of Fire-proof; it saved all that we intrusted to its care.

SAMUEL OBERDORFF.

GREAT FIRE AT LOCK HAVEN.

LOCK HAVEN, PA., December 10, 1862.

Messrs. Farrel, Herring & Co., Philadelphia:

GENTLEMEN—On Saturday last our town was visited by the largest fire we have ever had. Nearly all the business portion was destroyed—some *forty or fifty buildings*. The safe we had of your make stood the test nobly. Our books and papers are in a state of perfect preservation. We will send the safe to you and order one of larger size. We have all confidence in your safe and want no other make.

There was a cast or "chilled iron" safe of Troy manufacture all burned up in the same fire.

Yours truly,
WOODS & WRIGHT.

ANOTHER SAFE IN SAME FIRE.

LOCK HAVEN, PA., December 9, 1862.

Messrs. Farrel, Herring & Co., Philadelphia:

GENTLEMEN—About four o'clock on Saturday morning, the 6th inst., our town was nearly destroyed by fire, consuming about forty buildings, my store among the rest. I had one of your Fire-proof Safes in my jewelry store at the time, and it saved all my stock, books, papers, and money. Would like to know if you can fix the safe up if I send it to you, or what difference you will make one in exchange for a new one of same size.

Yours truly,
G. G. WEIDHAHN.

Plate No. 19.

No. 4 – Folding Door, with Banker's Chest.

Banker's Chest.

50 in. high, }
38 in. wide, } Inside.
18 in. deep, }

20 in. high, }
38 in. wide, } Outside.
18 in. deep, }

GREAT FIRE AT WELLSBORO'.

SEVEN STORES BURNED—FIVE OF HERRING'S SAFES TESTED!

WELLSBORO', PA., December 21, 1861.

Messrs. Herring & Co., New York:

GENTLEMEN—At the great fire which occurred here on the 18th December last my store, with a number of other buildings, was entirely destroyed. No fewer than seven places of business were burned out, and five of your safes were severely tested, in every instance saving their entire contents, to the complete and perfect satisfaction of the owners. Two of your Herring's Patent Champion Safes which were in my building remained there through the entire conflagration, and were not opened until the day after the fire. No water was thrown on the building. Everything in my safe, after the fire, was nearly as good as new. C. L. Wilcox also preserved all his books, papers, and money in two of your safes, both being in the same fire. William Roberts was also the fortunate owner of another of your Patent Champion Safes, which was severely tested, and saved completely his books, papers, and money. The result has given great satisfaction, and we want no safe but Herring's Champion. Please send me one, same size I last bought of you, immediately. Send by New York and Erie Railroad via Tioga depot.

JOHN R. BOWEN.

TWO MORE!

WELLSBORO', PA., January 6, 1862.

Messrs. Herring & Co., New York:

GENTLEMEN—At the time of the recent large fire in this place I was the fortunate owner of two of your safes, which were exposed to the said fire. The safes contained all my books, papers, and about two thousand dollars in bank-bills, which, it gives me pleasure to inform you, were preserved to my entire satisfaction.

Respectfully yours,

C. L. WILCOX.

ANOTHER!

WELLSBORO', PA., January 6, 1862.

Messrs. Herring, & Co., 251 Broadway, New York:

GENTLEMEN—It gives me pleasure to inform you that my books, papers, and about four hundred dollars in bank-bills, were preserved uninjured in one of your Patent Safes at the great fire which occurred here December 18, which destroyed a large portion of the business part of the town. I now have the utmost confidence in your safes, and would advise every man that has books and valuable papers to supply himself with one of Herring's Patent Champion Safes.

Yours, &c.,

WILLIAM ROBERTS.

FIVE SAFES IN THE FIRE AT WILLIAMSPORT, PA.

WILLIAMSPORT, PA., April 17, 1858.

Messrs. Farrel, Herring & Co., Philadelphia:

GENTLEMEN—Having examined five of your Herring's Patent Safes which passed through the ordeal of the burning of the large brick building situated in Williamsport, Lycoming county, Pa., recently occupied by J. H. Fulmer & Co. as a store, we cheerfully certify to the perfect safety of all combustible material contained in them; and from the evidences we thus have of the security of these safes we have no hesitation in stating that they are fire-proof. From our knowledge of the combustible material contained in said store and in the immediate vicinity of the safes, it was undoubtedly one of the severest tests to which they could have been subjected.

Signed,

ROBERT FLEMING,
DR. S. F. GREEN,
C. W. SCATES,
GEO. WHITE,
JOHN HAYS,
HUSTON HEPBURN,
WEBB, CANFIELD & CO.,
L. C. KINYON,
MAG. GEO. W. LENTZ,
WM. H. HAY,

J. H. FULMER & CO.,
THOS. SMITH,
H. A. FOULD,
WM. H. GIBSON,
THOS. LYMA,
S. JONES,
JUDGE JAS. ARMSTRONG,
DR. ANDREW KLETT,
THOS. THROP, P. M.,
C. H. BAEBLER.

THE GREAT FIRE AT OIL CITY.

FIVE OF HERRING'S PATENT CHAMPION SAFES SEVERELY TESTED.

NUMBER ONE.

OIL CITY BANK.

OIL CITY, PA., June 22, 1866.

Messrs. Herring, Farrel & Sherman, New York :

GENTLEMEN— The building in which the Oil City Bank had their office was entirely consumed in the destructive fire of May 26, which destroyed so many buildings. The bank was using one of your largest size Herring's Patent Champion Fire-proof Safes, with an inside Bankers' Burglar-proof Chest. The books, papers, and money which it contained were well preserved; every pen-mark is as bright as before the fire. This was a severe test of the fire-proof qualities of your safe, the fire being one of the hottest ever known in this region. Your safe has proved what you represented it to be perfectly fire-proof.

Respectfully yours,

JOHN B. CANBY, *Cashier*.

NUMBER TWO.

UNITED PETROLEUM FARMS ASSOCIATION.

OIL CITY, PA., June 22, 1866.

Messrs. Herring, Farrel & Sherman, New York :

GENTLEMEN—The great fire of May 26 completely destroyed our office. Our books, papers, and money were locked up in one of your Patent Champion Fire-proof Safes, with one of your Burglar-proof Chests across the bottom. They were all preserved in good condition. This safe was subjected to a tremendous test, as its exterior plainly shows, the iron being badly warped, the brass knobs and ornamental plates entirely melted off. A safe which will stand the test of such a fire as this one was can be truly recommended as perfectly proof against fire.

Respectfully yours,

ANDREW CONE,
General Superintendent U. P. F. Association.

NUMBER THREE.

Oil City, Pa., June 22, 1866.

Messrs. Herring, Farrel & Sherman, New York:

GENTLEMEN: Our store was totally destroyed in the large fire of May 26. The Herring's Patent Champion Safe manufactured by you which we had in use preserved its contents in excellent condition.

Respectfully yours,

BISHOP & DAWSON.

NUMBER FOUR.

Oil City, Pa., June 21, 1866.

Messrs. Farrel, Herring Co., Philadelphia:

GENTLEMEN: We were among the sufferers by the extensive conflagration which took place here May 26. The fire was the largest which ever occurred here, destroying half the business portion of the town.

The Patent Champion Safe of your manufacture saved the books, papers, and money which it contained in excellent condition; every word and line is perfectly legible. We can recommend your safes to business men.

Respectfully yours,

REYNOLDS, BRODHEAD & CO.

NUMBER FIVE.

Oil City, Pa., June 21, 1866.

Messrs. Farrel, Herring & Co., Philadelphia:

GENTLEMEN: The most destructive fire which ever occurred in this borough took place on the morning of May 26, which swept away a large portion of the business stores. I lost a large amount of property; however, I was the fortunate owner of one of your celebrated Patent Champion Fire-proof Safes, which contained my books and papers, with other valuables, which were saved in excellent order; it also contained a gold watch, with a hair chain, which came out, to my surprise, without a mark of fire.

Respectfully yours,

JOHN H. GOTSHALL.

FIRE IN GREENSBURG, PA.

Greensburg, Pa., Sept. 25, 1858.

Messrs. Farrel, Herring & Co., Philadelphia:

GENTLEMEN: One of the most destructive fires that has ever occurred in our place happened on Tuesday, the 22d instant, burning some twenty-five buildings. I had one of your Herring's Patent-fire Proof Safes in a building that was destroyed. The safe was subjected to an immense heat. It was taken from the ruins the following day, and the door, near the handle, was *still red-hot*. It contained books and a number of papers, loose and in bundles, which were not damaged in the slightest. It gives me pleasure to add to the accumulated evidences of the safety and reliability of your safes.

Yours truly,

J. TURNEY.

FIRE AT CARBONDALE.

CARBONDALE, Dec. 10, 1855.

Messrs. S. C. Herring & Co.:

GENTLEMEN—As I have one of your safes in my store that has passed through a most severe trial, I write you for the purpose of getting your opinion in reference to its future security. Does exposure to heat materially effect or destroy them for resisting a second exposure? If so, please write me your terms for exchanging for one of the same kind. This was purchased of you some two or three years since at a cost, I believe, of fifty-six dollars, and has well repaid its cost. Its trial has been as severe as one could often be exposed to. It stood in a large wooden store directly over the office; in the chamber was stored a large quantity of combustible materials, such as boxes, barrels, &c., which fell to the office below, and were consumed around the safe which contained my books, papers, and about two hundred dollars in money. On removing the safe, to the surprise of many, its contents were well preserved, having received no injury, with the exception of the leather binding to the books. I need not say to you that I consider your safes, in all ordinary cases, a perfect security; and would recommend to all about to purchase to try one of your manufacture, with the fullest confidence that in case of trial it will prove itself a perfect security against the destructive element.

Please write me at your earliest convenience.

Yours respectfully,
STEPHEN S. CLARK.

ANOTHER FIRE AT CARBONDALE.

CARBONDALE, January 11, 1859.

S. C. Herring & Co.:

GENTLEMEN—In the large and destructive fire at this place I had one of your safes, which was exposed to the severe test of heat eight hours, and, on opening, found our books and papers in a perfect state of preservation, and we now have them in use.

S. S. CLARK.

THE GREAT FIRE AT EASTON.

EASTON, May 2, 1855.

Messrs. Farrel & Herring, Philadelphia:

The Fire-proof Safe (Herring's Patent) which we purchased from you about six months since has proved itself fire-proof indeed. At the great fire in Easton on the night of the 21st of April last our carpenter-shop and all our lumber were consumed by the flames.

The safe stood in a part of the shop where it was surrounded by combustible materials, and was subjected to such an intense flame as to heat it to a white heat. It fell from the second story, and laid amongst the burning lumber for some considerable time before it could be removed; but when it was taken out and opened the next morning, the books, money, and loose papers in the pigeon-holes were all found uninjured.

Very respectfully yours,
E. & W. KELLER.

LARGE FIRE IN READING.

READING, PA., April 23, 1862.

Messrs. Farrel, Herring & Co., Philadelphia:

DEAR SIRS—On the 23d of March last we had the misfortune to have our Masonic Hall at this place burned out. We had one of Herring's Fire-proof Safes

Plate No. 20.

No. 4½— Folding Door, with Banker's Chest.

Banker's Chest.

56 in. high, }
38 in. wide, } Inside.
18 in. deep, }

20 in. high, }
38 in. wide, } Outside.
18 in. deep, }

in the Hall at the time. It saved our books, papers, and everything that was intrusted to its care. We are well satisfied with the result, and will send the safe down to you. Please send us another of the same sort, one size larger, as we now have the greatest confidence in your safes.

           FRED. LAUER.
           H. M. ALBRIGHT.
           TOBIAS BARTO.

FIRE AT RESACA.

          RESACA, PA., April 28, 1859.

Messrs. S. C. Herring & Co. :

GENTLEMEN—The Herring's Safe which we purchased from you a short time since was tested by fire on the 8th instant by the burning of our warehouse. It gives us pleasure to inform you that it preserved our books, papers, and money uninjured, although it was exposed to an intense heat for a long time. You will please make another safe of larger dimensions, as the other was too small to contain all our books.

    Yours truly,

           MILLER & MACKEY.

GREAT FIRE IN WILKESBARRE.

         WILKESBARRE, PA., June 3, 1859.

Messrs. Farrel, Herring & Co., No. 629 Chestnut street, Philadelphia :

GENTLEMEN.—On the night of the 30th and morning of the 31st May a fire broke out in this place, originating in my store, and consuming sixteen buildings in its ravages. The safe of your manufacture purchased from you a short time ago was in the hottest part of the fire for upwards of six hours, and was red-hot for a long time. I take great pleasure in informing you that my books, papers, &c., have since been taken from the safe in a good state of preservation. I shall purchase another of your safes as soon as I become located.

    Yours respectfully,

           ROBERT WILSON.

FIRE AT BLOSSBURG.

         BLOSSBURG, PA., April 23, 1862.

Messrs. Herring & Co. :

GENTLEMEN—Our store was entirely destroyed by fire on the 29th March last, and everything burned except the contents of your safe. The Herring's Patent Champion which we bought some four years ago held all our books, money, and valuable papers. It fell into the cellar with the burning timbers, and among goods of a very combustible character. It was in a very hot fire, and there remained until the fire exhausted itself, and nothing was left but the safe. The lock would not work, and we had to cut the door open. Our books, papers, and money were found all safe. Nothing damaged except the covers of the books, which were drawn by steam.

    Respectfully yours,

           GULICK & TAYLOR.

FIRE IN RUSHDALE.

Letter from a Banking House.

SCRANTON, PA., June 23, 1863.

Messrs. Herring & Co., New York :

GENTLEMEN— We send this day to the Metropolitan Bank $115 in currency that was taken out of one of your safes at Rushdale this morning, after a large store was burned, and heated your safe to a red heat.

The books and papers were all safe. If you desire to see and retain these bills, we have no objection.

Respectfully yours,

W. W. WINTON & CO.,
Bankers.

FIRE IN SHAMOKIN.

SHAMOKIN, PA., May 28, 1866.

Messrs. Farrel, Herring & Co., Philadelphia :

GENTLEMEN— I had the misfortune to have my store and stock of goods, which was large, burned on the 4th instant. All that was saved was my books, papers, and money, in one of your patent safes.

The fire was very large, consuming a block of buildings, and your safe was in the hottest part of the fire. I shall send the old safe to you and want you to send me one of next size larger.

Yours truly,

VALENTINE FAGELY.

FIRE IN TITUSVILLE.

TITUSVILLE, PA., March 22, 1865.

Messrs. Herring & Co. :

GENTLEMEN The large Herring's Patent Safe which we purchased of you last October and had in use passed through the late great fire at this place. The safe contained all our books, papers, and money at the time, and the contents were all well preserved, although the fire was very hot, burning a whole block of buildings.

G. S. WARREN & CO.

NEW JERSEY.

FIRE IN JERSEY CITY.

JERSEY CITY, February 19, 1852.

Silas C. Herring :

SIR— It gives us great pleasure to certify to the superiority of your safe, containing our books, papers, money, and watch-movements, which has just been recovered from the ruins of the fire caused by the burning of our store on the night of the 17th instant, by which it was exposed to an intense heat for twelve hours. Every line of the books and papers is perfectly legible, and the watch movements contained in the tin cases perfect and uninjured.

PROUD & BOWMAN,

Gold Watch-case Manufacturers, corner of York and Greene streets,
Jersey City, N. J.

ANOTHER FIRE IN JERSEY CITY.

JERSEY CITY, February 3, 1853.

Mr. Silas C. Herring:

SIR—It gives us much pleasure to say that a safe of your make was the means of preserving our books and valuable papers, together with a lot of silver spoons, forks, &c., from destruction by the fire that occurred in our store on the night of the 27th ultimo, at No. 46 Montgomery street. The fire commenced near the safe, which, owing to its situation on a wall, did not fall into the cellar, but was exposed to the full heat of the fire from the commencement, and when taken from the ruins had all the brass plates and knobs completely melted off.

R. B. EARLE & CO.

ANOTHER FIRE IN JERSEY CITY.

JERSEY CITY, N. J., January 21, 1860.

Messrs. Herring & Co.:

GENTLEMEN—The small safe which I purchased from you some time ago was in my large three-story brick building, which was entirely destroyed by fire on the 20th of August last. The safe was in the second story, in the middle of the building, and fell into the cellar, where it remained covered by the burning ruins for *three days*. On opening it, the contents, consisting of all my valuable papers and books, were found to be in a perfect state of preservation.

Respectfully yours,

S. W. BENNETT.

FIRE AT NEWARK.

[*From the Newark Daily Advertiser of Friday Evening, September 16, 1859.*]

This morning a Herring's Safe, which had been in the third story, and in the ruins all night, and in the hottest part of the flames, was taken out, and, on opening it, its contents (the books of Messrs Ward & Johnson) were found to be entirely preserved.

NEWARK, September 19, 1859.

Messrs. S. C. Herring & Co.:

GENTLEMEN—We take pleasure in stating that our books, papers, and money were preserved uninjured in one of your Patent Champion Safes at the burning of our moulding mill on the 15th instant, after being exposed to the fire for several hours.

WARD & JOHNSON.

ANOTHER FIRE IN NEWARK.

NEWARK, N. J., June 4, 1866.

Messrs. Herring, Farrel & Sherman:

GENTLEMEN—It affords me much pleasure to be enabled to say that the safe, which was of your make, and in my factory, No. 59 Railroad avenue, this city, at the time it was destroyed by fire in May last, although exposed to intense heat, and I am informed by one, a member of the Fire Department, that it was red-hot, yet the contents, books, papers, &c., were uninjured, not even the paint on the inside blistered. The result was so satisfactory that one of my neighbors purchased it for his own use; and as soon as my building is completed I will want another of the same sort.

Respectfully,

B. WEST.

FIRE AT PATERSON.

PATERSON, Jan. 2, 1857.

Silas C. Herring & Co. :

GENTLEMEN—It affords us great pleasure to inform you that the safe which we purchased of you some years since, and which was in our store at the time of its destruction by fire on the night of 30th December, 1856, has fully realized our expectations. It contained all our books and valuable papers, besides about eight hundred dollars in money, all of which were taken out of the safe, upon opening it, in just as good condition as when they were put in, with the exception of the covers of the books, which were curled by the steam.

VANDERVOORT & SNYDER.

FIRE IN BEVERLY.

BEVERLY, March 15, 1861.

Messrs. Farrel, Herring & Co., Philadelphia, Pa. :

GENTLEMEN—On the 7th inst. my three-story brick factory, together with its contents, was completely destroyed by fire. Fortunately I had my books and papers in one of your Herring's Patent Champion Safes, and I deem it but just to you to say that, to my surprise (judging from the intense heat, which showed its effects to a marked degree on the outside of the safe), everything came out in a perfect state of preservation - not a scrap of writing being destroyed. The safe was so situated as to expose it to the hottest kind of a test, it being red hot for a long time. I shall want another safe, and, of course, after this I can trust no other but one of this kind.

J. L. PRATT,
Proprietor Beverly Cutlery Works.

HENRY BAITOE, *Superintendent.*

We, the undersigned, cheerfully give our testimony of the truth of the above statement, having witnessed the exposed situation of the safe during the fire, and subsequent opening of the same.

C. J. HARBRICK.
W. H. MAKEPEACE.
C. W. HOWARD.
J. W. STOCKTON.
J. C. SKIPPER.

THE GREAT FIRE IN NEW BRUNSWICK.

NEW BRUNSWICK, N. J., January 18, 1862.

Messrs Herring & Co., No. 254 Broadway, N. Y.:

GENTLEMEN—At the recent extensive fire in our city, on Wednesday morning last, 15th instant, I was the fortunate owner of one of your Herring's Patent Champion Safes, which contained some books and a number of valuable papers. The heat in my store was very great, and the safe in the hottest part of it. I felt great interest in the safety of my papers, as a number of castings in my store, and within a few feet of the safe were melted; nothing, indeed, was saved in my building except the contents of your safe, which, I am happy to inform you, was completely preserved after a thorough roasting for some seventeen hours. The result has exceeded my anticipation and fully confirmed my confidence in the security of your Herring's Patent Safe. Please send me another of larger size, and refer all incredulous to my books and papers, which it gives me great pleasure to show.

Yours, &c.,

W. H. ARMSTRONG.

Plate No. 21.

No. 4½ – Folding Door, Banker's Chest, half Size.

Banker's Chest.

56 in. high,
38 in. wide, } Inside.
18 in. deep,

20 in. high,
19 in. wide, } Outside.
18 in. deep,

WASHINGTON, D. C.

FIRE IN WASHINGTON CITY.

WASHINGTON, D. C., May 28, 1860.

Messrs. Farrel, Herring & Co. :

On the 19th instant our planing-mill was totally destroyed by fire. We had one of your Patent Champion Safes, which we endeavored to rescue from the flames, but only succeeded in getting it in a position where the wind blew the flames directly on it. Yet, the books and papers entrusted to its keeping were found to be saved, although the fire was the hottest we have ever had in this place. We have no confidence in any other safes, and wish you to send us one of your make and a size larger.

Yours truly,

TRUMAN & DRAPER.

DESRUCTIVE FIRE IN WASHINGTON CITY.

WASHINGTON, September 16, 1865.

GENTLEMEN —The Herring Safe used in the office of our warehouses, destroyed by the disastrous fire of the night of the 8th instant, was subjected to as intense a heat as probably any safe will ever be subjected to in any fire—so intense that the brass knob and mountings of the exterior of the same were melted off, and the whole surface sealed and blistered as if it had been in a furnace ; and yet, when opened, the contents—books and papers—were found to be entire and uninjured.

This safe is now on exhibition in our warehouse on Seventh street, with the books and papers still remaining in it, just as it was when taken from the ruins. Merchants, bankers, and others interested in the protection of their books and papers are invited to call and examine it.

J. P. BARTHOLOW,

Agent for Herring's Safes, No. 558 Seventh street, Washington, D. C.

VIRGINIA.

FIRE AT RICHMOND.

RICHMOND, VA., November 2, 1859.

Messrs Knowles & Walford, Agents :

We take pleasure in adding to your long list of certificates our testimonials in favor of Herring's Patent Fire-proof Safes.

In the fire which consumed our Steam-sawing and Carpenter Shops on the night of the 29th of October last, we had one of Herring's Safes, and though exposed to intense heat (it was entirely red-hot on the out-side), from the burning floors and timbers which fell on it, on opening, the next day, we found no appearance to indicate that its contents had been near fire.

We shall order another from you in a few days, and use the old one at our sawing mill, near Mayo's Bridge, where you may refer customers who have any doubt about the fire-proof qualities of Herring's Safes.

JOHN & GEORGE GIBSON.

ANOTHER FIRE AT RICHMOND.

RICHMOND, VA., Aug. 6, 1860.

Messrs. Knowles & Walford, Agents:

GENTLEMEN—Allow us to add our testimony to the safety of Herring's Patent Fire-proof Safes. At the fire on the morning of the 4th, in which our factory and foundry, with contents, were a total loss, thanks to a Herring's Safe, our books came out as good as new, although the safe was subject to a red heat.

Respectfully yours,
LOWNES & COOK.

BURNING AND EVACUATION OF RICHMOND, APRIL 3, 1865.

NUMBER ONE.

RICHMOND, VA., May 15, 1865.

Messrs. Herring & Co., New York:

GENTLEMEN—The Herring's Patent Champion Safe which we purchased from you in the month of April, 1860, passed safely through the late terrible conflagration in this city, which destroyed over one thousand buildings, on the 3d of April last, upon its evacuation.

Our store was situated on Thirteenth street, and in the center of a vast field of conflagration. The safe was enveloped by flames and buried by the ruins. Our store was filled with groceries, tobacco, &c., while in the second story, immediately over the safe, were 200 bushels of rectified charcoal, making the heat so intense that when we attempted to get at the safe, two days after the fire, our workmen were compelled to desist.

We finally got at the safe on the fourth day after the burning, and, when opened, we are happy to testify that your safe proved itself a "fire-proof" indeed. Our books, papers, money, and entire contents were all right, and to our perfect satisfaction. We would inquire if the old safe is of any use to you, and how we can exchange for a new one. From our experience here, we would trust none but Herring's Champion.

WM. WALLACE'S SONS.

NUMBER TWO.

RICHMOND, VA., June 22, 1865.

Messrs. Herring & Co.:

GENTLEMEN—The building in which I had an office was totally destroyed by the terrible conflagration of the 3d of April last. Fortunately, I had one of your Herring's Patent Champion Safes in use, which entirely preserved my books, papers, &c.; every line is legible. The only injury is in the covers of the books being drawn by the steam.

Very truly yours,
S. P. LATHROP.

NUMBER THREE.

RICHMOND, VA., June 21, 1865.

Messrs. Herring & Co.:

GENTLEMEN—In reply to your inquiry as to how an iron safe of your make which I used stood the test of the great fire which occurred here in April last, I have to say that I opened it about ten days after the fire and found the contents in a comparatively good condition, the bindings of the books *only* being slightly injured. The papers and paper money which it contained are entirely uninjured.

Very respectfully, your obedient servant,
JOHN I. PAGE, JR.

Plate No. 22.

No. 5—Folding Door, with Banker's Chest.

56 in. high,	Banker's Chest.
14 in. wide, } Inside.	20 in. high,
18 in. deep,	14 in. wide, } Outside.
	18 in. deep,

NUMBER FOUR.

RICHMOND, June 5, 1865.

Messrs. Herring & Co., New York:

GENTLEMEN—We are happy to inform you that the contents of our safe, one of your manufacture, were very little injured by the great fire of 3d of April. The Burglar-proof in the bottom of the safe (inside) is also in good order, and was unlocked and locked with ease.

Very respectfully,

R. H. MAURY.

NUMBER FIVE.

RICHMOND, VA., May 30, 1865.

Messrs. Herring & Co., New York:

GENTLEMEN—I am pleased to testify to the superior quality of your "Fire-proof Safe." I was one of the sufferers by the recent conflagration in this city. My safe I bought some years ago stood the test on the memorable 3d of April last. After it had been encased in the ruins of my store for perhaps three weeks after the fire I opened it, through curiosity, not expecting to find the contents preserved; but, to my great gratification, everything was in a perfect state of preservation except the backs of my ledgers and journals, which were charred. If anybody wants to make a "safe" investment I would recommend him to patronize your concern.

I am, very respectfully,

GEO. L. BIDGOOD,

Bookseller and Stationer, Richmond, Va.

NUMBER SIX.

RICHMOND, VA., June 22, 1865.

Messrs. Farrell & Co., Philadelphia:

GENTLEMEN—The tremendous conflagration of April 3 in this city, at the time of the evacuation, completely destroyed my store. Your Herring's Patent Champion Safe which I had in use preserved its contents uninjured after being subjected to one of the most intense fires which ever took place in any country.

Yours truly,

GEO. RUSKELL,

No. 91 Main Street.

NUMBER SEVEN.

RICHMOND, June 9, 1865.

Messrs. Herring & Co., New York:

I hereby certify that, on opening the Herring Safe in my office, corner of Bank and Eleventh streets in this city, after it had been buried for three days in the ruins of the late conflagration, the books and papers therein were safe.

Yours, &c.,

JAS. M. TAYLOR.

NUMBERS EIGHT AND NINE.

RICHMOND, VA., June 21, 1865.

Messrs. Herring & Co., New York:

GENTLEMEN—In the conflagration which devastated the business portion of our city on the 3d of April last, our storehouse was destroyed.

Our books and papers were contained in two of your iron safes. They remained buried in the debris of the building for SIX WEEKS, and were subjected during the fire to a very *great heat*, owing to the combustible nature of some of our goods (oils and turpentine), as well as the large size of the house and quantity of material burned.

When opened the contents of the large safe, though injured, were in a great measure well preserved. In the other some papers were lost, but the majority of the contents saved. The vault inside the large safe proved an entire protector.

Very respectfully,
PURCELL, LADD & CO.

NUMBER TEN.

RICHMOND, July 3, 1865.

Messrs. Herring & Co.:

GENTLEMEN—We had the misfortune to be among the many sufferers in the immense conflagration which swept away a large portion of the business houses of this once prosperous city. We were the fortunate possessors of one of your Patent Champion Safes, which preserved our books and papers in excellent condition, although subjected to a severe test. This safe has done us good service and deserves great praise.

Respectfully yours,
ALVEY & LIPSCOMB.

NUMBER ELEVEN.

RICHMOND, VA., July 3, 1865.

Messrs. Herring & Co.:

GENTLEMEN—We take pleasure in informing you that one of your Patent Champion Fire-proof Safes was the means of saving our books, papers, &c., at the tremendous fire which took place here at the time of the evacuation of this city on the 3d of April last. The building in which we had our office was a large one, surrounded by some of the largest storehouses in the city which were filled with all kinds of combustible material, making the heat intense. The safe remained in the ruins about one week before it was opened. No water was thrown on the ruins at the time of or after the fire. When the magnitude of the fire is taken into consideration—over one thousand buildings having been destroyed with large stocks of goods in them, no means of moving safes from the ruins being at hand—it is indeed wonderful that any safe preserved its contents. Your safe has stood this severe test nobly, and we wish to give it the credit to which it is entitled.

Respectfully yours,
DAVID & WILLIAM CURRIE.

NUMBER TWELVE.

RICHMOND, VA., July 7, 1865.

Messrs. Herring & Co.:

GENTLEMEN—The great fire of April 3 destroyed the building in which I had my office. I was using one of your Patent Champion Safes, which preserved its contents in good condition, although subjected to a roasting which safes seldom receive in any fire, on account of the number of buildings and large quantities of combustible material stored in them. No water was thrown on the building or ruins, making the ordeal the more severe for the safe. It has sustained its heretofore well-earned reputation, and I take pleasure in adding my experience to those tested in other places.

Truly yours,
EUGENE CARRINGTON.

Plate No. 23.

No. 5—Folding Door, with Two Banker's Chests.

Banker's Chest.

56 in. high, } Inside.   24 in. high, } Outside.
44 in. wide,   14 in. wide,
18 in. deep,   18 in. deep,

Divided in the centre, making two complete Banker's Chests.

NUMBER THIRTEEN.

RICHMOND, VA., July 7, 1865.

Messrs. Herring & Co.:

GENTLEMEN— One of your Fire-proof Safes belonging to me was severely tested by the terrific conflagration of April 3. It contained my books, papers, &c., which were preserved in excellent condition; every line and word is legible. The heat of this fire probably was unparalleled in the world. Not a piece of wood was to be found in the ruins; even the ashes were totally burned up; in fact, safes were subjected to a furnace heat, as no water was thrown on the ruins. My safe remained buried in the ruins for about twenty-three days before opened.

Very respectfully,

W. F. PRICE.

NUMBER FOURTEEN.

RICHMOND, VA., July 10, 1865.

Messrs. Herring & Co.:

GENTLEMEN--You, of course, are aware of the immense destruction of buildings and property by fire on the memorable 30th of April last, when this city was evacuated. We were unfortunately among the sufferers. The building in which we carried on business is totally destroyed. Nothing remains but bricks; not a piece of wood is to be found on the premises, so clean did the fire burn. We had one of your Patent Champion Safes in use, which was the means of saving our books, papers, and money. You can judge of the heat to which this safe was subjected when we inform you that we did not dig it out of the ruins for six weeks after the fire, at which time it was still hot. You can make whatever use of this letter you please, believing that a safe which proved itself fire-proof in this terrible fire should have that credit to which it is fairly entitled.

Respectfully yours,

WILLIAM EUKER & BRO.

NUMBER FIFTEEN.

RICHMOND, VA., July 11, 1865.

Messrs. Herring & Co., New York:

DEAR SIRS—In compliance with your request we send you the following regarding the condition of one of your Herring's Patent Safes which was in our warehouse at the time of the great fire here. Our building was very large—say ninety feet square—built of brick, five stories in height, and was well filled with manufactured tobacco—say about four thousand boxes—all of which was burned to complete ashes, producing a very intense heat. Our safe had fallen one story and remained in an upright position. In consequence of the excessive heat produced by the burning tobacco we could not get to it for four days. When we did reach it we found the safe had been broken into and robbed of its contents after the fire. We had already taken the precaution to remove our most important books. We found some unimportant books, which had been thrown about by the robbers, the covers of which were damaged, but the contents were perfectly legible. We also saw some old checks which were scattered around that were perfect. The book-case was in perfect order, the varnish being uninjured. We feel sure that the heat in our building was certainly as great as in any other house, hundreds of kegs of nails having melted into a solid mass. The safe itself showed similar marks of the great heat, one of the handles being literally melted, and we are convinced that no other safe, when subjected to an equal test, has turned out in equally good order.

Yours respectfully,

HARVEY, JAMES & WILLIAMS.

NUMBER SIXTEEN.

RICHMOND, VA., July 12, 1865.

Messrs. Herring & Co.:

GENTLEMEN—The safe of your manufacture belonging to Messrs. Hitchcock & Osborn which was in our store at the time of the terrible conflagration of the 3d of April, and was not opened until Saturday, the 8th, preserved its contents in good condition; not only the books, but the loose papers, were all legible.

Respectfully yours,

KNOWLES & WALFORD.

NUMBER SEVENTEEN.

RICHMOND, VA., July 17, 1865.

Messrs. Herring & Co. :

GENTLEMEN—The Herring's Patent Champion Safe I had in use passed through the disastrous conflagration of April 3d, on the evacuation of this city, and was not opened until last Friday (July 14th). I am pleased to inform you that its contents were well preserved; everything is legible, which is truly wonderful, considering the severe test this safe was subjected to. This fire probably has no parallel for its tremendous heat in the history of such disasters.

Respectfully yours,

THOS. C. C. DREWRY.

NUMBER EIGHTEEN.

RICHMOND, VA., Aug. 21, 1865.

Messrs. Herring & Co.:

GENTLEMEN—We had one of your safes in the destructive fire of April 3, when the evacuation of this city took place. We had it dug out of the ruins *three weeks* after the fire. On opening it, our principal books were found in a legible condition.

Respectfully yours,

POWELL & VALENTINE.

NUMBER NINETEEN.

RICHMOND, VA., Aug. 21, 1865.

Messrs. Herring & Co.:

GENTLEMEN—Being one of the sufferers by the great fire of April 3, I desire to give you a statement in regard to the Herring's Patent Champion Safe I had in use in my jewelry business. After removing it from the ruins (being one week after the fire), we found the contents—consisting of jewelry, books, and papers—in my safe all right. This fire was one of the severest tests that was ever known.

Respectfully yours,

B. HEINRICH.

NUMBER TWENTY.

RICHMOND, VA., Aug. 21, 1865.

Messrs. Herring & Co.:

GENTLEMEN—The papers and valuables in my iron safe of Herring & Co.'s manufacture were not materially injured, though the fire around it was intense, on the 2d of April last, which destroyed so large a portion of the city.

My safe was exposed to as intense a heat and as severe a test as any other in the city.

Truly yours,

S. C. ROBINSON.

NUMBER TWENTY-ONE.

RICHMOND, VA., Aug. 22, 1865.

Messrs. Herring & Co.:

GENTLEMEN—The great fire of April 3, which occurred when this city was evacuated, destroyed our warehouse in which we had our office. We had in use one of your Patent Champion Safes, the safe being exposed. The building was a large one, and was completely gutted by the fire. The heat was severe. The safe contained our books and papers, which WERE PRESERVED in a partially damaged condition, the covers of the books being melted by the steam.

Respectfully yours,
DUNLOP, MONCURE & CO.

NUMBER TWENTY-TWO.

RICHMOND, VA., Aug. 23, 1865.

Messrs. Herring & Co.:

GENTLEMEN—The James River Manufacturing Company had one of your safes in use at the time of the great fire, which occurred April 3, when the city was evacuated. The books and papers which it contained were all preserved in good condition, the only injury being to the covers of the books being melted by steam. Some of them have been rebound and are now in use.

Respectfully yours,
C. B. BENTLEY,
Agent.

NUMBER TWENTY-THREE.

RICHMOND, VA., Aug. 23, 1865.

Messrs. Herring & Co.:

GENTLEMEN—The Herring's Patent Champion Safe we had in use in our store when the great fire of April 3 occurred, although remaining in the ruins *three weeks*, when opened the books and papers were in excellent condition, no sign of fire about them. When a safe preserves its contents in such an immense fire as this one was, it is, indeed, wonderful, and is entitled to be called fire-proof.

Respectfully yours,
CHARLES SCHUMANN & BRO.

GREAT FIRE AT PETERSBURG.

PETERSBURG, VA., March 13, 1854.

In the fire which destroyed our store and entire stock of goods on the night of the 3d of February last was one of Silas C. Herring's Safes, with Hall's Burglar-proof Lock, containing our books, papers, and a considerable amount in bank-notes and checks. Owing to the intense heat to which the safe was exposed, the brass knob which unlocks the door was melted off, and it could not be opened with the key, and had, therefore, to be forced open, which operation was effected with considerable difficulty.

On obtaining an entrance to the safe, the entire contents were found secure and uninjured by fire.

MORRISON & MARABLE.

HERRING'S FIRE-PROOF SAFES.

ANOTHER GREAT FIRE AT PETERSBURG.

PETERSBURG, VA., May 21, 1855.

Messrs. S. C. Herring & Co. :

Messrs. Falconer, Plummer & Co., in whose store the fire originated, had one of your Champion Safes, containing their books, papers, and six hundred dollars in bank-notes, which was in the hottest of the fire about twelve hours, and the contents were perfectly preserved to their entire satisfaction, as well as of the community at large ; and not a doubt now rests on the minds of any who saw the contents after the fire of the capability of your unrivaled safe to resist the most intense heat for almost an indefinite period of time.

Yours truly,
WATKINS, SON & CO.

GREAT FIRE AT LYNCHBURG.

LYNCHBURG, VA., Jan. 6, 1855.

Mr. S. C. Herring :

DEAR SIR —Early this morning our city was visited by a large and destructive fire, eight or ten buildings being consumed.

The occupant of one of them was fortunately provided with one of " Herring's Fire-proof Safes," which to-day has been taken from the ruins, and after giving it a little time to " cool off " was opened, and the books and papers found safe and in good order.

This is the first test applied to your safes here, and it is considered perfectly satisfactory.

Yours truly,
J. H. THOMPSON & CO.

ANOTHER GREAT FIRE.

FIRE IN LYNCHBURG.

LYNCHBURG, VA., August 29, 1865.

Messrs. Herring & Co. :

The most extensive and destructive fire that ever occurred in our city took place on Tuesday night, 25th inst. Four large grocery and commission houses, with their valuable contents, were entirely destroyed. I take pleasure in informing you that your Herring's Patent Champion Safe has again stood the test and came out more than triumphant. After unlocking my safe and taking out a few of my books and papers, I was so closely pressed by heat, smoke, and falling bricks that I was not able to empty the safe ; it fell into the cellar, and, after remaining there four days among the burning remains of fifteen hundred boxes of tobacco, it was opened to-day. With the exception of slight injury to the books and papers, which did not render them illegible or valueless, the contents of the drawers, consisting of money and other valuables, were entirely uninjured. I do not recollect of an instance where a safe subjected to such intense heat for so long a time preserved its contents so perfectly.

Yours truly,
GEORGE STEPTOE.

ANOTHER IN SAME FIRE.

LYNCHBURG, VA., August 30, 1865.

Messrs. Herring & Co. :

GENTLEMEN—Your Herring's Patent Champion Safe preserved the papers left in our safe when our store was destroyed by the recent great fire, which was the largest that ever took place in our city.

Truly yours,
H. H. ROSE & CO.

Plate No. 24.

No. 6--Folding Door, with Banker's Chest.

61 in. high, ⎫
54 in. wide, ⎬ Inside.
19 in. deep, ⎭

Banker's Chest.
20 in. high, ⎫
54 in. wide, ⎬ Outside.
19 in. deep, ⎭

FIRE AT NORFOLK.

NORFOLK, VA., January 17, 1856.

By request of Messrs. Rowland & Brothers we this day attended the opening of one of Herring's Fire-proof Safes, which was in the fire of December 7, belonging to Messrs. Adams & Co.'s Express, and found the papers and contents in a perfect state of preservation. It was, in our opinion, as severe a test as could be had. A large four-story building was entirely destroyed, and the safe remained the whole time surrounded by fire and subject to an intense heat for forty days before being dug from the ruins.

Signed,
GEO. F. ANDERSON.   C. HALL.
WM. D. REYNOLDS.   A. B. McLEAN.
MILES DAVIS.   W. W. JACOBS.

I am fully satisfied with the manner in which the above safe preserved its contents.

A. A. COWDRY,
Agent Adams & Co.'s Express.

ANOTHER EXTENSIVE FIRE IN NORFOLK.

NORFOLK, VA., August 14, 1866.

Messrs. Herring & Co., New York city:

GENTLEMEN—About two months since a fire broke out in a large frame building of which nearly every part was of North Carolina pitch-pine, or light wood. My safe—one of your make—was in one corner of the building, and, unfortunately, the hook company, in pulling the timbers down, pulled all the heavy upper timbers immediately over the safe. In this way it was, with heavy timbers above and below, in a cherry-red heat for about twenty hours. In fact, so great was the heat that every particle of brass melted from it. When it was taken out I feared the opening, as in it were papers of some forty or fifty thousand dollars value, besides many private papers of value; but I was agreeably surprised to find them all entire. The books were injured in the binding, and the veneering of the safe on the inside warped. I have sent it to you with the hope that you will put it in order for me at as moderate a charge as you can, or exchange it for me. Please let me hear from you on receipt of this.

Yours very respectfully,
W. W. PIERCE,
303 *Post-office, Norfolk, Va.*

FIRE IN BOTETOURT COUNTY.

JUNCTION STORE, BOTETOURT CO., VA., April 20, 1855.

Messrs. Knowles & Walford:

Our frame storehouse and stock of goods at this place were totally destroyed by fire on Monday night, the 26th of February last.

In the fire was one of Silas C. Herring's Safes, weighing 1,340 pounds net, and it contained our valuable books and papers, and the books, notes, and funds of the Clinton Savings Bank, in all amounting to a very large sum. Also, there was one pound of powder tied up in a piece of paper, which one of our young men had placed in the safe and neglected to remove.

The safe was in the hottest part of the fire about six hours, and was red hot. One of the feet or rollers was considerably damaged by the fire, and the back and one side are a little sprung. After the safe had become quite cool on the outside it was opened, and its contents, though warm, were in perfect good order and condition. We now have the books in regular use, and they are not in the least drawn or warped.

We would not now be afraid to risk the safe in any fire produced by the burning of a house.

JONES & MAYS.

I was present when the Junction Store was destroyed by fire, and also opened the safe with the key, and do hereby certify that the above statement made by Messrs. Jones & Mays is true and correct in every particular.

WM. B. CARPER.

NORTH CAROLINA.

FIRE AT GREENVILLE.

GREENVILLE, PITT CO., October 25, 1858.

S. C. Herring & Co. :

Our County Court-house was destroyed by fire on the night of January 9, 1857. All the books and papers of the County Clerk's Office were totally destroyed. At that time I was Sheriff of the county, and had one of your Fire-proof Safes, which contained my valuable papers and money, in the second story of the building, which fell with the burning ruins, and was subjected to an intense heat. On opening its contents were uninjured.

Our county would not have met with any loss had they had the same security.

Yours respectfully,

ABRAM COX.

FIRE AT MAGNOLIA.

MAGNOLIA, N. C., August 1, 1859.

Messrs. S. C. Herring & Co. :

GENTLEMEN—On the 5th of March last our storehouse was destroyed by fire, and one of your Herring's Safes was in the ruins twelve hours, in a most intense heat. On opening it, we found the contents perfectly safe, and wish you to send us another of larger size, for we would not be without one of your safes, and consider them superior to any other.

Yours truly,

MERRIMAN & NEWBURY.

GREAT FIRE AT LOUISBURG.

LOUISBURG, N. C., January 9, 1861.

Farrel, Herring & Co., Philadelphia, Pa.:

GENTLEMEN—On the night of the 20th December, 1860, a fire occurred in our town, destroying the whole business portion of the place, except two stores. We had one of your Patent Champion Safes, purchased about one year ago, which contained all the books and papers belonging to the firm ; also the private papers and notes of our Mr. Ballard. From the position in which the safe stood during the fire it was subjected to an immense amount of heat, lasting several hours ; and, although it was supposed by many of our citizens that the contents were destroyed, everything came out satisfactory, the binding on the books being the only part affected. We have ordered another from your agent.

B. T. BALLARD & CO.

LOUISBURG, N. C., January 12, 1861.

Messrs. Herring & Co.:

A large fire occurred in this town on the night of the 28th December, 1860. My office was on the second floor of a large wooden two-story building. I had in my office a safe of your make, which fell with the building, and remained exposed to all the fire. The heat melted off the brass knobs and plates. I had removed my papers, but left one accidentally, which I found in a perfect state of preservation. I am perfectly satisfied that it would have preserved my papers, as the wood framing inside the safe was uninjured, except by stain (by the glue and steam, I presumed).

I am sure the safe was all that it was represented to be.

Respectfully yours,
J. J. DAVIS.

FIRE AT NEWBERN.

NEWBERN, N. C., January 29, 1861.

Messrs. Herring & Co. :

GENTLEMEN— Your letter of the 24th inst. is at hand, and in reply would inform you that the safe we purchased of Messrs. Farrel, Herring & Co., of Philadelphia, has given entire satisfaction, and we would take pleasure in recommending them to all who want protection from fire for books and valuables. The safe was red-hot when taken from the ruins, and after cooling some time we discovered smoke coming out of the safe, and were fearful that our books and papers were on fire, and consequently went to work to ascertain if such was the case, but were highly gratified to learn that all our books, money, &c., were safe. We wish to know if you will exchange with us, and, if so, what you will allow us for the one taken from the ruins. We are very much in want of a safe, but do not feel able to purchase one at present.

Yours respectfully,
C. A. HART BROS. & CO.

P. S.—We have a photograph of the ruins that shows the safe as it was opened, and, if you wish, will send you one.

SOUTH CAROLINA.

GREAT FIRE AT CHERAW, MAY, 1852.

CHERAW, S. C., May 26, 1852.

John Farrel, Esq., 34 Walnut street, Philadelphia:

DEAR SIR—Yours of the 21st inst. is at hand. The telegraph reported me as burned out, but I fortunately escaped.

Mr. W. L. J. Reid had one of Herring's Safes in his store ; the safe was of small size, about 700 lbs. ; the store was of pitch-pine ; I stood by and saw the safe taken from the ruins ; the safe was opened by the key with as much ease as if it had not been exposed to the fire. It contained Mr. Reid's books and papers and about $200 in bank bills ; everything was in good order, except the binding of the books, which was injured somewhat, I think, by water poured upon the safe to cool it.

I have one of Herring's Safes in my store, for which I paid $150 ; I would not take $1,000 dollars to be without it. I have full confidence in their being an entire protection against fire. Several of our merchants lost their books, but none having the Salamander Safe.

Respectfully yours,
D. MALLOY.

THE SAME SAFE IN ANOTHER FIRE.

CHERAW, S. C., Friday, Sept. 1, 1854.

Mr. Silas C. Herring, No. 135 Water street, New York:

DEAR SIR—On the 18th of March last my store was again destroyed by fire, and again your safe preserved my books and papers without damage, save the leather binding a little stained.

Please send me another of your safes as soon as possible. Send me about No. 7, Herring's Patent. I have full confidence in your safes after two trials, and want no other.

Yours respectfully, W. L. J. REID.

HAYNES STREET FIRE, CHARLESTON.

CHARLESTON, S. C., May, 1854.

To S. C. Herring, Esq., New York:

DEAR SIR The "Salamander Safe" which we procured of you was in our store, No. 29 Haynes street, at the time of its destruction by fire on the 18th of April last. The entire building, together with seven others in the same block, was destroyed. This safe was buried among the ruins for several days, when it was dug out, and, very much to our surprise, from the combustible nature of our business (wholesale drugs and medicines), on opening it, found its contents to be in *perfect order;* and from this we are satisfied that your safes are entitled to public confidence. You will please ship us another of the same size at once, and oblige

Very respectfully yours,
P. M. COHEN & CO.,
Importers of Drugs and Medicines, 29 Haynes street.

THE GREAT FIRE AT NEWBERRY, JUNE 18, 1866.

NEWBERRY, S. C., September, 1866.

Messrs. Herring, Farrel & Sherman, 251 Broadway, New York:

GENTLEMEN—In the great fire at this place on the 18th of June last our store, with many others, was entirely destroyed. The Herring's Safe purchased from your house some years ago was in the fire and had a very severe roasting, as several thousand pounds of bacon were burned near it. The safe remained in the burning embers for two days before it was taken out and opened. The safe was filled with our books, papers, &c., and had carried them safely through the conflagration. Everything came out nicely and in an unexpected state of preservation. Nothing was injured.

Truly yours, LOVELACE & WHEELER.

FIRE AT NEWBERRY.

NEWBERRY, S. C., September, 1866.

Messrs. Farrel, Herring & Co.:

GENTLEMEN—We can testify with pleasure, in reply to your inquiries, that your safe faithfully performed its duty in the severe trial to which it was put during the great fire in this place on the 18th of June last. Our building was large and burned with great heat. The safe was taken from the burning pile on the second day, and its contents were perfectly sound. This safe of your manufacture was purchased some seven or eight years since, and has not only proven its genuine quality as a fire-proof, but has also shown that age does not depreciate it.

Respectfully yours,
MARSHALL & BRO.

Plate No. 25.

No. 6—Folding Door, with Banker's Chest in centre.

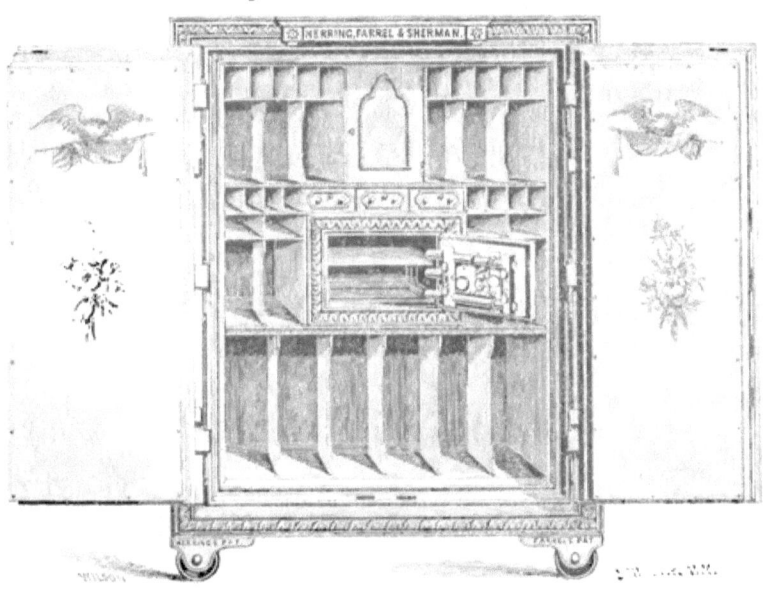

Banker's Chest.

61 in. high, 51 in. wide, Inside. 19 in. deep,

20 in. high, 24 in. wide, Outside. 19 in. deep,

GREAT FIRE AT ABBEVILLE.

ABBEVILLE, S. C., August 21, 1858.

Messrs. Farrel, Herring & Co., Philadelphia:

GENTLEMEN—The close attention which our affairs have required since the fire has hitherto prevented us from writing you about the safe. On the occasion of the fire, 19th July, by which we suffered a large loss, our store, with a number of other buildings, was consumed. The Herring's Patent Safe manufactured by you, which we had in the store, was exposed to a most intense heat, as is well attested by the effects on its strong iron frame, which, from its flaked and scaly appearance, looks as though it had been heated for a long time in a furnace. The safe, with heaps of molten glass and kegs of nails *fused into a mass*, fell into the cellar, surrounded by burning materials, and there was suffered to remain (as the contents had been removed before the fire reached us) until the 2d August—fourteen days afterward. The difficulty in cutting it open with the best tools that could be procured convinced us of its power to resist the attempts of burglars, and when it was opened, we found the interior, to the astonishment of all, entirely uninjured by fire. This test has so fully convinced us of the capabilities of your safes that we would not part with the one we have in use for a large sum, were we debarred the privilege of getting another.

Respectfully yours,
R. H. WARDLAW & SON.

FIRE AT UNIONVILLE.

UNIONVILLE, S. C., October 12, 1860.

Messrs. Farrel, Herring & Co., Philadelphia:

GENTLEMEN—On the morning of the 11th of July last a tremendous fire occurred here, destroying an immense amount of property. I had one of your Patent Safes in use in my store, and had removed it to the middle of the street, which is very narrow. The buildings on both sides of the street, extending two squares, were burned to the ground, which created an intense heat, so much so that the safe became red-hot. It contained my books and papers, amounting to twelve thousand dollars, and five thousand dollars in bank-bills, which were found, on opening the safe, to be in as good a state of preservation as when put into it.

Yours truly,
THOMAS McNALLY.

GREAT FIRE IN DARLINGTON.

OFFICE OF THE "SOUTHERNER,"
DARLINGTON, S. C., September 26, 1866.

Messrs. Herring, Farrel & Sherman,
New York city:

GENTLEMEN—Your favor of the 20th ultimo inquiring how the Herring's Patent Safes stood the test in the fire at this place last March is at hand. I reply as follows: I had all of my papers, books, money, and other valuables in one of your safes, and received them after the building burned down in excellent order. The safe was subjected to a great trial, having no protection of brick around it. It was a large building made of our pitch-pine timber, and resisted the intense heat well and satisfactorily.

Respectfully,
J. M. BROWN,
Proprietor of the "Southerner."

THE BURNING OF COLUMBIA.

COLUMBIA, S. C., August 19, 1865.

Messrs. Herring & Co., New York:

GENTLEMEN—The Herring's Patent Safe that the firm of Falls & Kinard bought of you in 1856 was in use by me at the time that Sherman's army entered this place. My store, with many others, was entirely destroyed by fire. The safe was in the hottest of the fire; but all my books, papers, &c., which were left in the safe, were well preserved. When I get started again in business I shall want another, as this fire has demonstrated that they are fire-proof.

Yours respectfully,
J. H. KINARD,
Formerly Falls & Kinard.

GEORGIA.

FIRE AT ATLANTA.

ATLANTA, GA., November 15, 1855.

S. C. Herring & Co.:

GENTLEMEN—Permit me to inform you that on Sunday night, the 7th of January last, my three-story brick building, used as an auction and commission house, on Alabama street, was set on fire by an incendiary and was consumed in a few hours, in which was one of your small safes, measuring 23 by 19 inches, containing a small case of notes, twelve or fifteen bank-bills, and a handful of gold and silver coin in an earthen bowl; all preserved perfectly sound and whole, the bills not even scorched, but very damp. The safe being on the second floor and falling into the basement on a pile of green oak wood, remained there until the whole of the wood, as well as that of the building, was consumed; it was perfectly *red-hot*. At length, by my consent, the captain of the fire company cooled it off and rolled it out. Its contents were then examined and resulted as above stated.

The above statement can be substantiated by five hundred persons if necessary. You are at liberty to use the above in any way you may think proper.

STEPHEN J. SHACKELFORD.

THE GREAT FIRE AT ATLANTA.

ATLANTA, GA, November 23, 1859.

S. C. Herring & Co., No. 251 Broadway, New York:

GENTLEMEN—The small safe which I purchased of you some time since was in my large two-story wooden building, which was burned at the great fire here on the 16th instant. The safe was red-hot, and on opening it the next morning I found its contents, which consisted of silver, two hundred dollars in bank-bills, with other papers, all safe and sound.

J. S. SHACKLEFORD, *Auctioneer.*

ANOTHER.

ATLANTA, GA., December 2, 1859.

S. C. Herring & Co.:

GENTLEMEN—I had one of your safes in the late disastrous fire which occurred here on the 16th ultimo. My books and papers, also some ninety watches and watch materials, were in the safe, and although the safe was under an intense heat for a long time, upon getting it open I found everything saved to my entire satisfaction. I can, therefore, readily testify to the perfect fire-proof quality of Herring's Patent Safe, and it is with much pleasure I give you these facts.

Yours respectfully,
RILEY S. BAKER.

AND ANOTHER.

ATLANTA, GA., December 10, 1859.

S. C. Herring & Co.:

This is to certify that I have owned and used one of Herring's Patent Fire-Proof Safes for some time, and at the late destructive and extensive fire in the city of Atlanta, on the night of November 16, 1859, the safe had valuable papers in it. It was in my law office, on the second floor, in Mr. Markham's large three-story brick building, and during the fire and burning of said building the safe fell into the cellar, and there remained imbedded in the midst of the hot ruins for *eighteen days and nights*. It was then taken out, and when opened (although the safe, in its present injured condition outside, was unfit for further use) the papers were all safe.

This severe test convinces me that it is decidedly best to have "Herring's Patent Fire-proof Safes" for the protection of papers against fire.

JARED IRWIN WHITAKER.

AND ANOTHER.

ATLANTA., GA., December 15, 1859.

Messrs. Farrel, Herring & Co., Philadelphia:

GENTLEMEN—In the late disastrous fire I had some two hundred dollars in one of Herring's Patent Safes, and after the fire, when the safe was taken from the ruins and opened, to my most complete satisfaction not a dollar was injured. I feel completely satisfied that the genuine Herring's Patent Safes are perfectly fire-proof; for any safe that could stand the heat this one did, lying among burning spirits, liquors, oils, &c., for hours, must unquestionably be the most perfect protection against fire ever manufactured. I make this statement most cheerfully, and remain,

Yours truly,
J. A. GIBSON.

STILL ANOTHER.

Messrs. S. C. Herring & Co.:

GENTLEMEN—The Herring's Patent Champion Safe I bought of you about one month ago was in the fire on the night of the 16th instant, in a large two-story wooden building, and on opening it I found the books and papers all right. I have since bought another of your agents, W. Herring & Son.

Respectfully yours,
F. H. COLEMAN.

FIRE AT AMERICUS.

AMERICUS, GA., May, 1857.

Messrs. S. C. Herring & Co.:

GENTLEMEN—It gives me pleasure to inform you that the safe which I purchased of you last September has proved what you represented to me when I bought it—

perfectly fire-proof. The safe was exposed to all the heat made by the destruction of my warehouse by fire on the night of the 12th inst., and when recovered from the burning ruins and opened I found all my books, papers, and about seven hundred dollars in bank-bills, in good condition; the only damage done to my books was in the binding, which was curled by the steam.

C. C. GREENE.

ANOTHER FIRE AT AMERICUS.

SAVANNAH, GA., June 6, 1860.

Messrs. Herring & Co., Manufacturers of Herring's Patent Champion Safes, New York:

GENTLEMEN— The banking office of the Bank of Savannah, at Americus, Ga., was destroyed by fire on the 12th day of May, 1857. In this office was one of Herring's Champion Safes, containing money, books, and valuable papers. The safe, though severely tested, preserved its contents, to our great satisfaction, entirely uninjured.

Very respectfully yours,
G. C. CARMICHAEL.

GREAT FIRE AT MARIETTA.

PHILADELPHIA, June 2, 1857.

Messrs. Farrel & Herring, 34 Walnut street:

GENTLEMEN— In answer to your inquiry about your Herring's Patent Safe, purchased by Mr Edward Denmead, of Marietta, Ga., I would state that I was at that place on the night of the great fire, April 14th last, which destroyed most of the business part of the town, and had deposited some papers and property of my own in Mr. Denmead's safe before the fire took place. The fire was very destructive; Mr. Denmead's warehouse was swept away and nothing saved but the CONTENTS OF YOUR SAFE, which passed through the conflagration, preserving the books, money, &c., of the owner (including my own papers, &c.), uninjured by fire. Bank notes which were taken from the safe when it was opened were as good as new; nothing, in fact, was damaged except the backs of the books and some wax seals, which were curled and melted by the steam.

Yours respectfully,
THOMAS STEWARDSON, M. D.,
No. 13 Prune street.

FIRE AT MONROE.

MONROE, GA., April 27, 1858.

Messrs. Herring & Co.:

GENTLEMEN— On the 7th of April, 1857, a destructive fire occurred in this place, which destroyed our store and contents, with the exception of our books, money, and valuable papers, which were preserved in one of your Herring's Patent Champion Safes. We cheerfully recommend to all having valuables to preserve from fire to inclose them in one of Herring's Patent Safes.

T. & J. A. COOPER.

FIRE AT COLUMBUS.

COLUMBUS, GA., October 26, 1859.

S. C. Herring & Co.:

On the 7th of June last our cotton warehouse was consumed by fire. In the

Plate No. 26.

Double Fire-Proof Safe.

All sizes made double, as per above illustration, and recommended for situations of extra hazard.

second story of the building was our office, in which we had one of your safes, containing valuable books and papers. Immediately under our office cotton was stored, tiered fourteen feet high. The floor of the office soon gave way and the safe fell upon the burning cotton below, resting on two tiers of cotton eighteen to twenty inches apart, fronting a door which opened into a cotton yard, through which came currents of air, producing a perfect furnace-heat for eight consecutive hours. We were so certain that the contents of the safe were destroyed that we did not remove it from the rubbish of the burning ruins for several days. But on removing and opening it, we found, to our great surprise, that all was safe, no papers or books injured. We have just ordered another through your agent.

Your obedient servants,

ALLEN & CAMAK.

GREAT FIRE IN GREENSBORO.

GREENSBORO, GA., June 6, 1860.

Messrs. Herring & Co. :

GENTLEMEN—In the extensive fire which occurred in this place on the night of the 26th of March last our store was entirely consumed. We had in the store one of your Champion Safes, in which were deposited our money, books, and papers. After the fire was over it was taken out of the ruins and opened. All the contents were preserved, the binding of the books only being curled by steam. We think them now the best safes made.

Very respectfully,

JOHNSON & PORTER.

GREAT FIRE IN CUTHBERT.

CUTHBERT, GA., August 15, 1860.

Messrs. Herring & Co., New York :

GENTLEMEN—On the night of the 14th of July last a fire occurred here which consumed several buildings—eight or ten. Of the number was our office. In it was the safe recently purchased from you, containing our books and valuable papers. The fire originated about 11 o'clock. Our safe was removed from the ruins of our office about 8 or 9 o'clock A. M., and was opened about 6 o'clock in the evening, before it was entirely cold. We found the contents slightly injured, but the books and papers are legible. You will please send us another safe, a duplicate of the other, since we are unwilling to risk our books and valuable papers in our office unless protected in a safe.

Very respectfully,

DOUGLASS & DOUGLASS.

FIRE AT ALBANY.

ALBANY, GA., December 3, 1860.

Messrs. Herring & Co. :

GENTLEMEN—I have been using one of your Patent Safes, which was purchased by Mr. Crummy some three years ago. The safe has recently passed through a fire here. The fire was so hot that it burned off one of the handles. The lock could not be unlocked with the key, so we were obliged to cut the door to pieces in order to get inside. On opening the safe, all the money and papers were safe. The covers of the books were melted off, but the writing and figures were all plain and good as before the fire. Will the safe, repaired, be good for another fire ?

Yours respectfully,

L. C. SHAW.

We, the undersigned, citizens of Albany, Ga., certify that, on the morning of the 19th of November last, Mr. L. C. Shaw had his building on Washington street entirely destroyed by fire; that we examined the safe of Herring's make, No. 16,174, while the remains of the fire were still burning, and before the safe itself was cool from the heat. We examined the papers taken from it afterward, and found them, together with books, money, &c., all uninjured and sound.

    Y. G. RUST, Agent Marine Bank.
    SIMS & RUST, Warehouse & Commission Merchants.
    JOHNSON & CO.,   "   "   "
    C. W. RAWSON, Merchant.
    NELSON TIFT, Cashier Branch Merchants & Planters' Bank.
    T. J. FLINT, Southwestern RR. Agent.
    JOHN A. DAVIS.
    E. RICHARDSON, P. M.
    HINES & HOBBS, Attorney-at-Law.
    ROBT. A. BEERS, Merchant.
    JAMES M. MERCER, Mayor.
    D. A. VASON, Attorney-at-Law.

FLORIDA.

GREAT FIRE AT TALLAHASSE, 1843.

At the destruction of a large number of warehouses in this city, one of these safes, purchased and used by the Florida Life and Trust Insurance Company of that place, although buried in the burning fire for a long time, effectually preserved its contents and delivered them up unscathed.

FIRE IN PILATKA.

                                          PILATKA, FLA., March 19, 1859.

Messrs. S. C. Herring & Co., No. 251 Broadway, New York:

GENTLEMEN—In justice to the merits and virtue of Herring's Patent Fire-proof Safes, we would inform you that on the 31st day of January last our warehouse, wharf, and store were entirely destroyed by fire.

Fortunately, we had our principal books, papers, and a large amount of money, secured in one of your safes, which, although it was exposed to the most intense heat for upward of five hours, surrounded by the most fierce and consuming fire, and putting your safe to the most severe test as to its fire-proof qualities, we are happy to say it proved itself worthy of the highest recommendation. Our books, papers, &c., which it contained, were preserved uninjured.

We gladly and gratefully tender our testimonial to the many already published toward giving the Herring Safe the credit and confidence it truly merits.

                                    Very respectfully,
                                                      TEASDALE & REID.

FIRE AT KEY WEST.

                                          KEY WEST, FLA., June 1, 1859.

S. C. Herring & Co.:

GENTLEMEN—On the 16th ultimo, during the great fire at this place, our store was entirely destroyed. We had one of your safes, but removed the books and papers,

Plate No. 27.

IMPROVED PATENT BANKER'S SAFE.

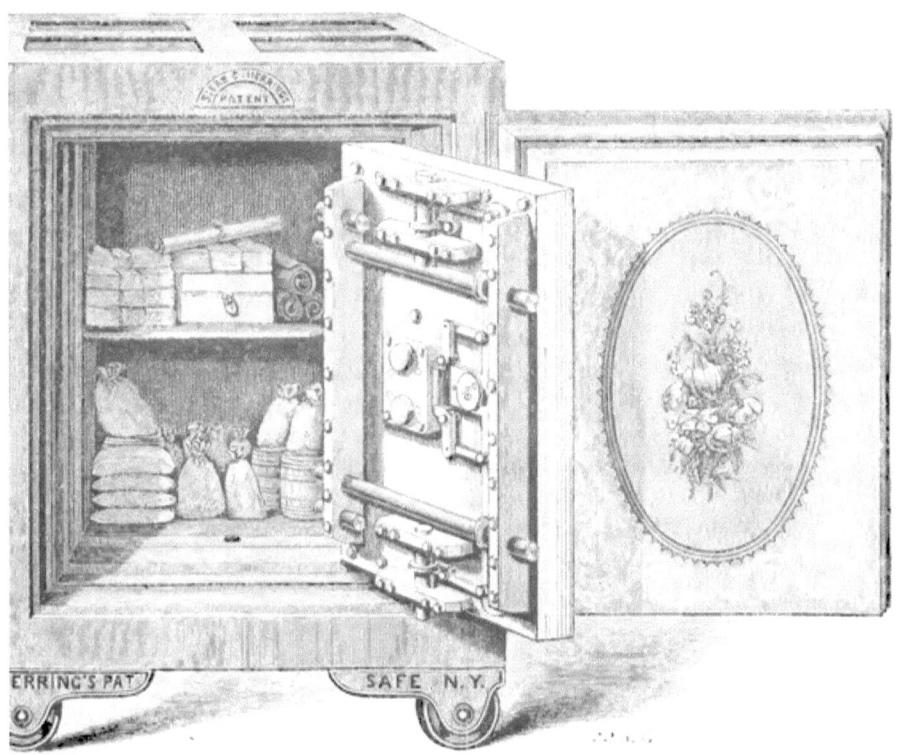

This safe is composed of two complete safes, one to protect against Burglars, the other against Fire, and one placed within the other. Our idea of a Fire and Burglar safe is, to make the two separate and complete in themselves, and then unite them, so that each has its own protection independent of the other.

except one small book, which, on opening the safe, after being in the ruins *eighteen hours* in a heat that melted the brass plates and knobs, we found in a good state of preservation, without any injury save that caused to the binding by steam. I was so well pleased with your safe that I shall procure another as soon as possible.

Yours respectfully,

C. & E. HOWE.

GREAT FIRE AT MARIANNA.

MARIANNA, FLA., November 4, 1859.

Messrs. Herring & Co.:

GENTLEMEN—On the 28th of October our town was visited by a very destructive fire and the largest one which has ever taken place here, destroying a whole block of the finest stores in the place. I had a Herring's Patent Safe in use, which was subjected to a most intense heat and fell into a cellar below. After removing from the ruins and opening it, the contents were found to be wholly uninjured. I would here remark that they truly merit the title of the Champion Fire-proof Safe. You will please ship me another immediately, as I do not consider my books, papers, and money secure without one.

Respectfully yours,

D. B. LESLIE.

ANOTHER LARGE FIRE IN MARIANNA.

MARIANNA, FLA., August 18, 1860.

Messrs. Herring & Co.:

GENTLEMEN—We certify that we have owned and used one of Herring's Patent Fire-proof Safes for some time, and that at the fire here on the 11th of July last it was situated in the second story of a large new building, from where it fell to the first floor and remained in an intense heat for some three or four hours. Two days afterward we got it out, and, upon opening it, we found all of our papers (a large number) and what money was in it well preserved. Although the safe is unfit for further use, we are satisfied it is fire-proof beyond a doubt.

McCLELLAND & BARNES,

Attorneys-at-Law.

P. S.—Forward us another similar to the first, as we consider one indispensable.

McC. & B.

ANOTHER.

MARIANNA, FLA., August 18, 1860.

Messrs. Herring & Co.:

GENTLEMEN—At the time of the destruction of our store by fire, which occurred on the night of July 14, we had one of your Patent Safes in use, which preserved its contents. Please ship us another one, a size larger than the other.

Respectfully yours,

PARKER & KING.

GREAT FIRE AT JACKSONVILLE.

JACKSONVILLE, FLA., October 2, 1866.

Messrs. Herring, Farrel & Sherman, New York:

GENTLEMEN—At the destructive fire in this place on the 11th of March last I had one of your safes, bought some years ago. The building in which my safe was located was of pitch-pine and made a very hot fire.

The brass knobs and plates in front were melted off, and the iron severely burned and weakened by the heat.

On opening the safe, though the contents showed marks of severe exposure, my books were all saved in good condition. Please send me another of same size; and in event of another visitation I shall be all ready for it.

Respectfully yours,

THEO. HARTRIDGE.

ALABAMA.

FIRE AT MOBILE.

MOBILE, ALA., April 5, 1855.

Mr. S. C. Herring:

DEAR SIR—I had at the destruction of my office by fire on the 21st day of March last a safe of your make, which was exposed to intense heat. Although I had removed most of my books and papers before the fire reached my counting-room, enough was left in the safe to test its fire-proof quality; and upon opening the safe, the papers left within were found perfectly legible, and the mahogany book-case in a good state of preservation.

I intend to purchase another of your Improved Patent Champion Safes of a larger size.

W. M. PLEASANTS.

ANOTHER FIRE AT MOBILE.

MOBILE, ALA., Aug. 1, 1856.

S. C. Herring & Co.:

GENTLEMEN—My store was destroyed by fire. I was fortunate enough to have my books and papers in one of your safes, and I am happy to say that they were preserved uninjured. I consider your safes superior to all others, and shall not feel safe without one of your make.

ROBT. S. KIRK.

GREAT FIRE AT MOBILE.

MOBILE, ALA., March 15, 1860.

Messrs. O. Mazange & Co., Agents Herring's Champion Safes:

GENTLEMEN—We take pleasure in stating that the Herring's Patent Champion Safe purchased from you last year has been the means of preserving our books, papers, &c., from the fire at the destruction of our office and building this morning. When we opened the safe, after the fire, we found its contents in as good condition as when put in last evening. The safe was exposed to a severe test and proved its fire-proof qualities. We cheerfully recommend Herring's Patent Champion Safes to our friends and the public.

MALONE & FOOTE.

Plate No. 28.

No. 1—Folding Door, Triple Safe.

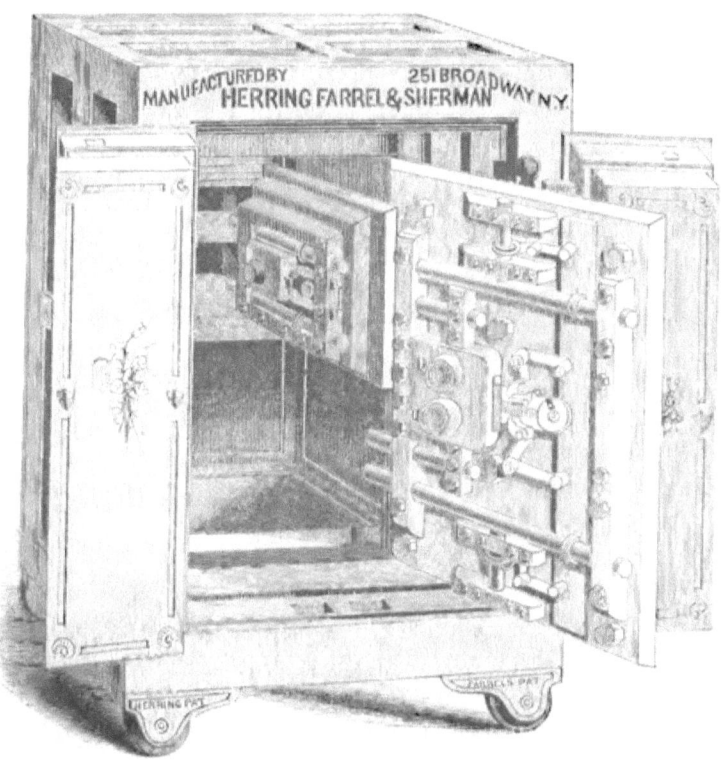

Or "BANKER'S SAFE" with BANKER'S CHEST inside.

	Banker's Chest.
38 in. high, ⎫	19 in. high, ⎫
21 in. wide, ⎬ Inside.	21 in. wide, ⎬ Outside.
16 in. deep, ⎭	16 in. deep, ⎭

This safe is made like "Improved Banker's Safe," represented on Plate 27, with an additional Banker's Chest or "Burglar-proof," inside.

FIRE AT MOBILE.

MOBILE, ALA., Jan. 22, 1861.

Messrs. Herring & Co.:

GENTLEMEN—The Herring's Patent Champion purchased of your house, through your agents, passed through the large fire which occurred here on the 31st of December last, falling through the ruins below, where it remained for two days. When opened the contents were found in a perfect state of preservation. The woodwork was in perfect order. We have ordered another safe from your agent, feeling perfectly satisfied of the fire-proof qualities of your make.

KELLY, JACKSON & CO.

ANOTHER IN SAME FIRE.

MOBILE, ALA., Jan. 23, 1861.

Messrs. Herring & Co.:

GENTLEMEN—We had one of your Patent Champion Safes in the late fire here. It stood in the second story of a three-story brick building. The safe fell in the ruins, and, when removed and opened, the contents were removed in a perfect state of preservation; nothing inside was injured. We cheerfully give you this certificate, being satisfied that your safes are fire-proof.

MILLER, WEAVER & CO.

LARGE FIRE AT GREENVILLE.

GREENVILLE, ALA., January 31, 1861.

Messrs. Herring & Co.:

GENTLEMEN—When my office, with other buildings, was burned on the night of the 27th inst., I had two of Herring's Safes in it. The papers and the bank-bills in one were well preserved. The other safe fell into the cellar and was exposed to great heat for about nine hours. The books and papers in this, though damaged by steam, can be used by rebinding the books.

JOHN K. HENRY.

ANOTHER IN SAME FIRE.

GREENVILLE, ALA., January 31, 1861.

Messrs. Herring & Co.:

GENTLEMEN—I had a No. 7 safe in the late fire at this place, which contained my papers; and, although the safe was subjected to an intense heat for hours—melting off the handles and plates—everything was faithfully preserved. It was all that it was recommended to me to be.

When I resume business I will want another one.

C. L. LINTHICUM.

THE TWO GREAT FIRES IN GREENVILLE.

GREENVILLE, ALA., August, 1865.

Messrs. Herring & Co., New York.

GENTLEMEN—On the 27th of January, 1861, at which time all communication with your city was cut off, our town was visited by a severe conflagration, which destroyed some thirty odd buildings. Unfortunately, my building was consumed with the others, and was in the business center of the town. One of the two safes which we bought from you in the summer of 1860 passed through the fire, preserving its contents—consisting of books, papers, and money—in good order. The other safe we managed to get out of the building without being much injured, and it was in the second large fire with which our place was visited on the 15th of September following. This great fire was much larger than the former, destroying the whole business part of the town. The safe that we rescued from the first fire passed through the second one, and again we were indebted to its good qualities for the preservation of our books and papers, though in the hottest of the fire.

Besides the above two safes, the following gentlemen, who were burned out, also had your safe in use at the time of the fires, all of which resisted the flames and saved their books and papers: Deming Estate, J. H. Dunklin, N. B. Rowe, and others.

Yours respectfully,

D. G. DUNKLIN.

GREAT FIRE AT BELL'S LANDING.

CLAIRBORNE, ALA., August 24, 1857.

Messrs. S. C. Herring & Co.:

GENTLEMEN—The Herring's Patent Champion Safe we purchased of you was exposed to a very hot fire in the burning of our warehouse at Bell's Landing. The only damage to any of the contents of the safe was the melting of the glue on the binding of the books. The papers, money, bank-bills, and everything in the safe, were uninjured, except the binding, as above stated.

We will state that we believe your safes of great value to business men.

Yours respectfully,

J. W. & W. P. LESLIE.

MISSISSIPPI.

FIRE AT COLUMBUS.

COLUMBUS, MISS., September 2, 1859.

Messrs. S. C. Herring & Co.:

GENTLEMEN—We have now in use in our office one of Silas C. Herring & Co.'s Fire-proof Safes which was burned in the fire that consumed the store of Jonathan Decherd & Co., in 1854, and never scorched a paper in it.

IRION & LOVE,

Attorneys-at-Law.

DESTRUCTIVE FIRE AT MARION STATION.

MERIDIAN, MISS., August 1, 1866.

Messrs. Herring, Farrel & Sherman, No. 251 Broadway, New York:

GENTLEMEN—At the destructive fire which took place at Marion Station on the 11th of January, 1860, our store, with others, together with our entire stock of goods, was burned to the ground. We had one of your Patent Champion Safes at the time, which contained our books, valuable papers, and nearly five thousand dollars in money. The safe was found in the ruins after the fire was over, and was red-hot. When it was opened, much to our agreeable surprise, we found money, books, and everything all safe. We are much pleased with the result, and when we visit New York will call on you and buy another safe of the same kind.

Yours truly,

O. & J. ROSENBAUM.

FIRE IN BRANDON.

BRANDON, Miss., September 20, 1866.

Messrs. Herring, Farrel & Sherman:

It may be interesting to you, and I think it may be a benefit to the business men, to inform you that the Herring's Patent Safe bought of you in 1856 was in my store at the time it was burned July, 1863, and contained all my valuable papers. The building was one hundred and forty-five feet long, two stories high, and made a very severe fire. The safe was red-hot, and after recovering the same from the ruins, on opening it I found everything in good order. You will ship me another of a larger size, and also one of same size to Messrs. Harper & Shelby of this place.

Respectfully,

R. MAXEY.

LOUISIANA.

FIRE AT NEW ORLEANS IN 1842.

At the burning of the large warehouse of Messrs. J. W. Stanton & Co., the public prints thus notice:

"We saw the Salamander Safe yesterday taken from the ruins of the store occupied by J. W. Stanton & Co. The books and papers it contained were in as perfect a state of preservation as they would have been had there not been a fire within ten squares of them. The oil and candles in the store of Stanton & Co. made about as comfortable a fire as we desire to see.—*N. O. Picayune.*

GREAT FIRE AT NEW ORLEANS, 15TH AND 16TH FEBRUARY, 1850.

NEW ORLEANS, LA., February, 1850.

DEAR SIR—I take great pleasure to inform you that I had in my office, No. 58 Camp street, a Patent Safe made by S. C. Herring, purchased from you, which was, in my opinion, subject to as severe a test as any safe during the great fire on the night of the 15th and 16th instant. So severe did the fire rage around this safe that the brass plates and knobs were all melted off. On opening the safe the contents were found to be in a perfect state of preservation. A quantity of banknotes and title-deeds were taken out after the fire in as perfect a state as they were when I put them in my safe before the fire took place. So well am I satisfied that I shall, as soon as I obtain another office, purchase from you one of the same kind, or perhaps larger, and can confidently recommend your safes as truly fire-proof. You may refer to me any one wishing to inquire respecting the above facts.

Yours very respectfully,

EDWIN FERGUSON.

To Mr. FREDERICK CAMERDEN, New Orleans, *Agent for Herring's Safes.*

BURNING OF THE ST. CHARLES HOTEL.

NEW ORLEANS, April 23, 1851.

John Farrel, Agent for Herring's Safes, Philadelphia:

DEAR SIR—As regards the large Herring's Safe which I had in my jewelry store

AND ANOTHER.

NEW ORLEANS, April 15, 1854.

Mr. Silas C. Herring:

SIR—On the evening of the 15th of March last our store, No. 36 Natchez street, was consumed by fire. In our counting-room, on the second floor, we had one of your safes, which contained most of our books, valuable papers, and several hundred dollars in bank-bills. The safe remained in the flames from two o'clock at night until five o'clock the next day. The brass knob, door-plate, and other metal ornaments, were melted off; and, when opened, we found all the books, papers, and money in perfect order; the backs of some of the books being slightly charred. Since the fire we have purchased another of your Improved Patent Double-flange Safes from Mr. George W. Sizer, your agent here.

(Signed)

C. & G. B. TATE.

ANOTHER FIRE AT NEW ORLEANS.

NEW ORLEANS, August, 1854.

Mr. Silas C. Herring:

SIR—We deem it a duty to hand you a certificate of the fact that our books, papers, &c., were preserved in one of Herring's Patent Safes in the great fire on the 5th inst., on Magazine and Tchoupitoulas streets. The safe was exposed to the most intense heat for several hours, and, when opened, its contents—consisting of books, papers, &c.—were found to be as perfect as when first put in.

Yours respectfully,

J. M. SAVAGE & CO.

FIRE AT NEW ORLEANS.

NEW ORLEANS, Sept. 15, 1857.

Messrs. S. C. Herring & Co.:

GENTLEMEN—Our store and contents were entirely destroyed by fire on the morning of July 8th, 1857. A portion of our books and papers, along with a large amount of cash, was deposited in the new safe purchased from you, which was subjected to an intense heat for several hours, and, when opened, the contents were in a perfect state of preservation.

ELLIOTT & CO.,
Per WM. B. CLARK.

FIRE AT NEW ORLEANS.

NEW ORLEANS, Dec. 13, 1861.

Messrs. Herring & Co.:

GENTLEMEN—In the fire which occurred on the evening of the 7th inst. at the store of Mr. E. Blessey, No. 74 Poydras street, consuming the building, with all its contents, the undersigned had one of your Fire-proof Safes. Upon examining the same, after an exposure of over twelve hours to the most intense heat, its contents were found to be in a well-preserved condition; and I have much pleasure in thus adding my testimonial to the many you have already received relative to the fire-proof qualities of your Champion Safes.

I am, gentlemen, yours respectfully,

EDWARD C. CARTWRIGHT.

AND ANOTHER.

NEW ORLEANS, April 15, 1854.

Mr. Silas C. Herring:

SIR—On the evening of the 15th of March last our store, No. 36 Natchez street, was consumed by fire. In our counting-room, on the second floor, we had one of your safes, which contained most of our books, valuable papers, and several hundred dollars in bank-bills. The safe remained in the flames from two o'clock at night until five o'clock the next day. The brass knob, door-plate, and other metal ornaments, were melted off; and, when opened, we found all the books, papers, and money in perfect order; the backs of some of the books being slightly charred. Since the fire we have purchased another of your Improved Patent Double-flange Safes from Mr. George W. Sizer, your agent here.

(Signed)

C. & G. B. TATE.

ANOTHER FIRE AT NEW ORLEANS.

NEW ORLEANS, August, 1854.

Mr. Silas C. Herring:

SIR—We deem it a duty to hand you a certificate of the fact that our books, papers, &c., were preserved in one of Herring's Patent Safes in the great fire on the 5th inst., on Magazine and Tchoupitoulas streets. The safe was exposed to the most intense heat for several hours, and, when opened, its contents —consisting of books, papers, &c.—were found to be as perfect as when first put in.

Yours respectfully,

J. M. SAVAGE & CO.

FIRE AT NEW ORLEANS.

NEW ORLEANS, Sept. 15, 1857.

Messrs. S. C. Herring & Co.:

GENTLEMEN—Our store and contents were entirely destroyed by fire on the morning of July 8th, 1857. A portion of our books and papers, along with a large amount of cash, was deposited in the new safe purchased from you, which was subjected to an intense heat for several hours, and, when opened, the contents were in a perfect state of preservation.

ELLIOTT & CO.,

Per WM. B. CLARK.

FIRE AT NEW ORLEANS.

NEW ORLEANS, Dec. 13, 1861.

Messrs. Herring & Co.:

GENTLEMEN—In the fire which occurred on the evening of the 7th inst. at the store of Mr. E. Blessey, No. 74 Poydras street, consuming the building, with all its contents, the undersigned had one of your Fire-proof Safes. Upon examining the same, after an exposure of over twelve hours to the most intense heat, its contents were found to be in a well-preserved condition; and I have much pleasure in thus adding my testimonial to the many you have already received relative to the fire-proof qualities of your Champion Safes.

I am, gentlemen, yours respectfully,

EDWARD C. CARTWRIGHT.

TEXAS.

FIRE AT INDIANOLA.

March 29, 1854.

We do this day certify that a safe manufactured by Silas C. Herring did, on the 27th day of July last, insure our books and papers from the effect of a late fire, and that we will conscientiously recommend them to any one who may desire a Fire-proof Safe.

BALDRIDGE, SPARKS & CO.

FIRE IN HOUSTON.

Houston, April 18, 1859.

Messrs. S. C. Herring & Co.:

GENTLEMEN—You have doubtless heard of the conflagration in our town on the night of the 8th of February last, which consumed our entire building and a large amount of goods. We had our books and papers in one of your large Herring's Patent Safes, and they came out in perfect order.

W. R. WILSON.

THE GREAT FIRE IN HOUSTON.

Test No. 1.

Houston, Texas, June, 1860.

Messrs. Herring & Co., No. 251 Broadway, New York:

GENTLEMEN—In the great fire which occurred at this place on the 9th of March last I had the misfortune to be among the sufferers. The fire was the most extensive that has ever occurred in this city or State. The safe of your manufacture which I purchased from you was in my building and exposed to all the severity of this terrible ordeal. After the fire was over, and I succeeded in getting the safe from the burned district, it was opened and the entire contents were found to be all safe. I am well pleased with the result, and consider this trial of far greater severity than safes are liable to be exposed to. Everything in my safe—consisting of papers, &c.—was not only in good order, but a watch which I had put inside for safe keeping was as good as new.

DAN M. CUTTER.

Test No. 2.

Houston, Texas, March 21, 1860.

Messrs. S. C. Herring & Co.:

GENTLEMEN—At the time of the great fire here, on the 9th instant, my building was entirely consumed. I had one of Herring's Safes in use, which contained my books, papers, and some gold and silver. After getting the safe out of the ruins I found the contents all in good order, with the exception of being slightly steamed, and think it will stand another test.

J. S. TAFT.

THE GREAT FIRE IN DALLAS.

Dallas, Texas, July 10, 1860.

Messrs. Herring & Co., No. 251 Broadway, New York:

GENTLEMEN—You have doubtless heard of the disastrous conflagration which devastated our town on the 8th of this month, destroying every business house, and almost sweeping Dallas from the face of the country.

I had one of your Patent Champion Safes in my store at the time, which contained all my books, papers, money, &c. The safe was surrounded by heavy burning timbers for a long time, and was as hot as fire could make it. The safe was in the fire until the next day, as we could not reach it on account of the heat. Judge of my surprise when we got it open to find everything all safe—not a paper scorched and nothing injured but the melting of the varnish and glue in the backs of the books. One of my neighbors—who had a safe of another New York make—was not so fortunate; he came to me after the fire and said: "I have been deceived in my safe, it is good for nothing. When you go to New York buy me one of Herring's." You will please ship one immediately, say a size smaller than mine, care R. & D. G. Mills, Galveston.

Yours truly,

E. M. STACKPOLE.

ANOTHER SAFE IN THE SAME FIRE.

HERRING'S PATENT ALONE TRIUMPHANT!

DALLAS, TEXAS, September 2, 1860.

Messrs. Herring & Co., New York:

GENTLEMEN—Your esteemed favor of the 23d of July came to hand some time ago; my absence and the fire delayed the answer.

My brother, who was here during the fire, told me that at the commencement of the same he put all my books in the safe, having full confidence in it; and as nearly every building on the square was destroyed, this was very fortunate, otherwise they would probably have been lost. The leather on the books simply was affected; the paper scarcely touched, and the writing all perfectly legible.

Please send me another of your ninety-dollar safes, care of Kauffman & Kloener, Galveston, on the same terms I bought the other.

Yours respectfully,

A. SHIREK.

P. S.—Some safes of other make tested here have proven to be worthless.

ARKANSAS

FIRE AT LITTLE ROCK.

LITTLE ROCK, ARK., January 7, 1865.

F. W. Roberts, Agent Herring's Safes:

DEAR SIR—About the year 1859 we purchased one of Herring's Safes. On the morning of the 1st inst. we were so unfortunate as to be burned out. Our business being drugs, the fire was very hot around the safe for over five hours, and we are happy to inform you that it stood the test to a charm, having preserved its contents in perfect order; but the door is sprung and the spring of the lock was so much out of order that we had to remove the iron plate over the lock and cut the lock open; so as the safe now is we cannot use it. Now we wish to know what to do—whether you can send us a new door that would fit it, or whether the safe will have to be forwarded to you?

Yours respectfully,

KENNEAR & HUGHES.

MISSOURI.

FIRE IN ST. LOUIS, APRIL 9, 1848.

[*Extract of a letter received from J. H. Alexander & Co.*]

ο ο ο ο ο ο ο We had a pretty clever fire here some two weeks since, which tested two of your safes which we sold. They were in the front part of the second story of a four-story stone building, filled with merchandise and liquors, and fell through to the first story, and, when cooled off, were unlocked, and the inside found to be all O. K. It has given very general satisfaction here.

The above safes belonged severally to Messrs. Matthews & Co. and Mr. R. B. Catherwood, who thus, though everything else was destroyed, through this instrumentality, preserved their invaluable books and papers.

GREAT FIRE IN ST. LOUIS, 17TH AND 18TH MAY, 1849.

FIFTEEN BLOCKS OF BUILDINGS AND FROM $3,000,000 TO $5,000,000 WORTH OF PROPERTY DESTROYED!!!

In the ruins of the above great fire no less than TWENTY Herring's Safes lay buried, and for confirmation of the very satisfactory result, the public are referred to the letters here following, and the subjoined well-known firms themselves who were the owners of the Safes then exposed to the fire. Suffice it to say, that although so many were subjected to that fiery trial, not a single loss occurred:

ST. LOUIS, Mo., July, 1849.

Mr. S. C. Herring:

DEAR SIR—The safe which we purchased of you some time last year was in our store during the "great conflagration" at this place in May last; and it gives us much pleasure to say that, though very much exposed, and we did not get at it until it had been in the fire some forty-eight hours, when finally dug out from the ruins of our building—contrary to our own forebodings and the prophecies of those who saw it before opening—it delivered up its contents in excellent order; not only were the books and money all safe, but loose papers, lying as much exposed as they well could be inside, were as bright as when put in. We must also say, in justice to the safe, before concluding, that we cannot conceive the possibility of a safe being more exposed, even in that great fire, than this, our own, was; as it fell from the back part of our office floor (second story), and when first got at was completely imbedded in the red-hot limestone. The outside appearances testify but too well to the intense heat to which it was subjected; not only are the maker's name-plate and the brass knob completely melted, but the heavy iron rollers on the bottom of the safe are run down into strings.

Yours, &c.,
S. & J. HAMILL,
Late Hamill, McMechan & Co.

ANOTHER IN SAME FIRE.

ST. LOUIS, Aug. 10, 1849.

Messrs. J. H. Alexander & Co., Agents for Herring's Safes:

GENTLEMEN—Having bought of you one of Herring's Safes, it may be important to persons wishing to get a safe that they can rely upon as secure to know the condition of such as were exposed to the great fire of the 17th May last. We removed the safe from the ruins on the morning of the 19th at a late hour, and

Plate No. 30.

Looking into the Vault of Brown, Brothers & Co.,
WALL STREET, NEW YORK.

The above is a bird's-eye view of the interior of BROWN, BROTHERS & CO'S great Vault recently erected in their new Banking House, and considered one of the best in the world.

It is entered through two sets of massive doors, each two inches thick, of Wrought and Patent Crystallized Iron, making 4 inches in all. Inside can be seen five large Banker's Chests; each one is no less than *four inches thick*, of solid wrought iron and "*Spiegel Eisen*," the best burglar-proof yet made.

Each Safe is secured by two Double Combination Bank Locks, capable of hundreds of millions of changes.

from the appearance it presented we expected to find the books and papers it contained to be useless, if not entirely destroyed. But on forcing it open we found that the greatest injury to the books was in the parting of the covers. The papers are all legible, and will serve for future reference as well as if no accident had occurred. We are well satisfied with the test in this as well as in other instances; and the best evidence of the confidence we place in them is the fact of having ordered, through you, another of the same description.

Yours respectfully,

HELFENSTEIN, GORE & CO.

AND ANOTHER.

St. Louis, August 2, 1849.

Messrs. J. H. Alexander & Co.:

GENTLEMEN—The safe (Herring's) we purchased of you was in the fire of the 17th May last, and upon opening it we found our books and papers in a good state of preservation.

Your obedient servants,

KEITH, RAY & CO.

ANOTHER.

St. Louis, July 27, 1849.

Messrs. J. H. Alexander & Co.:

GENTLEMEN—At your request we send you an account of the contents of our safe, purchased of you. On the night of the fire we took out our books and filled it with unimportant papers; it fell with the floor into the cellar on a load of charcoal, and lay there for a week before we got it out. When it was got out we applied the key and opened it as easily as ever, and found our papers fully legible, though somewhat parched from being so long in the fire. As it is, we use it as usual.

Yours truly,

JOHNSON & MANNY.

In addition to the above the subscribers would refer to the following gentlemen, all of whom had these safes exposed in the fire at that time:

JACARD & CO.,	THOS. B. DUTCHER & BRO.,
EDWARD MEAD,	EDGELL, PEASLY & CO.,
M. LAFLIN,	P. WILSON & CO.,
D'OEUCH, PELLOUX & CO.,	EDWARD MATTHEWS & BRO.,
D. W. GRAHAM,	BERTHOLD, EWING & CO.,
MATTISON & PRESTON,	FERDINAND KENNETT,
L. PECHMAN,	JAS. E. WOODRUFF & CO.,
St. Louis Floating Dock and Insurance Co.,	W. T. REYNOLDS.

ANOTHER FIRE AT ST. LOUIS, DECEMBER 16, 1849.

[From the New York Journal of Commerce.]

FIRE AT ST. LOUIS.—On the 16th inst. a fire broke out in the large four-story brick building on Locust street, between Water and Main streets, owned by Lewis A. Labaume; the edifice, about fifty feet front, was divided by a center wall into two tenements. The first floor was occupied by Messrs. J. H. Alexander & Co., produce and commission merchants and agents for the sale of Safes; the second floor by J. E. Woodruff & Co., Messrs. T. B. Dutcher & Bro., Mr. C. Adolphe Low, and Messrs. R. M. Funkhouser & Co. Not an article of any kind was saved

—in fact, no one entered after the fire was first discovered. The above parties have lost all their books and papers, unless the iron safes in which they were deposited have resisted the action of the fire.

[*Extract of a letter from J. H. Alexander & Co.*]

St. Louis, December 22, 1849.

Mr. S. C. Herring, New York :

DEAR SIR—We had the misfortune to have, on the evening of Sunday last, 17th inst., our store, with its entire contents, destroyed by fire—of which fact you are aware by telegraph. There were FOUR of your safes, which contained books and papers, in the fire, and *all* of them turned out *first-rate*.

The safes here named belonged to the parties referred to in the above notice, and it will be seen that the iron safes here mentioned did effectually resist all the action of the fire.

LARGE FIRE AT ST. LOUIS, MAY, 1852.

[*From the Missouri Republican, May 26.*]

A SECURE SAFE.—The safe owned by Messrs. McMehan & Co., and taken from the ruins of the building destroyed night before last on the levee, is a good sample of what a good safe should be—an unconquerable phœnix, which will rise the more triumphantly from its ashes at every new conflagration. This safe, one of Herring's, passed unscathed through a former ordeal, although subjected for many hours, it is said, to a perfect flood of flames. In this instance the worst materials, as bacon, liquors, dry pine timbers, &c., contributed their fury to the flames which enveloped the safe; yet, on its being opened, the papers and books of Messrs. McMehan & Co. were comparatively in excellent condition—no material injury had been done them. Speak to us about safes that carry out the object of their construction like this. Messrs. J. H. Alexander & Co., the agents for Herring's safes, finding that our dumb and wrought iron hero has proved a good and faithful servant, will, if they can, get it back, roll it into sheets and hang out the banners on their outward walls, on Pine street, where it may celebrate its own glory.

GREAT FIRE AT ST. LOUIS.

St. Louis, September 22, 1856.

Messrs. Roberts and Davis :

GENTLEMEN—It gives us great pleasure to inform you that the safe purchased of your manufacture, Herring's Patent, by Mr. Bailey, last summer, was taken from the ruins of the fire this morning. The safe was almost red-hot when we reached it, after being exposed seven hours, and from the outside appearance, the brass name-plate being melted off, we supposed it was entirely destroyed. We were very much surprised to find, upon opening it, the wood-work in good order, our books and papers perfectly legible, also bank bills all safe and sound.

C H. BAILEY.
MOSES ELEY.

ANOTHER GREAT FIRE AT ST. LOUIS.

Messrs. Roberts & Davis :

GENTLEMEN—The Herring's Patent Champion Safe of your manufacture, which we purchased about five months ago, was in our building at the time of its destruction, on the night of the 19th inst. We had removed the greater portion of our books before the fire reached us, but left one or two inside purposely to test the security of the safe. After FOURTEEN HOURS OF SEVERE ROASTING we found the INTERIOR OF THE SAFE, upon opening, perfectly sound, the varnish not being taken off, the BOOKS PERFECTLY LEGIBLE. We cheerfully recommend your CHAMPION SAFE to the public, and as soon as we get a new location shall require another safe, and none other than HERRING'S PATENT CHAMPION will do us.

We remain yours, &c.

W. O. WHEELER & CO.

FIRE AT TRENTON.

TRENTON, Mo., January 3, 1864.

Messrs. Pratt & Fox, St. Louis:

GENTLEMEN—On the 11th instant the building in which our office was situated, which was a large two-story brick, containing two stores, printing office, four law offices, and boot and shoe shop, was totally consumed by fire.

The large iron safe (Herring's Patent) which our firm bought of your house a few years ago went through the fiery trial and came out unscathed. It not only brought its contents through safely, but we have it still in use apparently as good as ever.

Respectfully yours,

SHANKLIN & AUSTIN.

TENNESSEE.

CANNON'S STORE, SEVIER CO., E. TENN., Feb. 2, 1861.

Herring & Co.:

GENTLEMEN— My store was burned on the night of the 14th of January last. I had my notes and cash in the safe I purchased from you September 29th, 1860, which were preserved uninjured. My store was a two-story frame building. We did not get the safe out until the building was entirely destroyed. The safe when taken from the ruins was red-hot all over. I wish to know if it will be safe to risk it in another fire.

Yours,

W. H. CANNON.

OHIO.

THE GREAT FIRE AT CLEVELAND.

[*From the Tribune of November 2, 1854.*]

THE CLEVELAND FIRE.—The safe of J. Morrison, banker, which came safely out of this great fire with $20,000 of bank notes unharmed, was one of Herring's make, despite the indirect claim laid to it by other parties. Here is the evidence:

[*Extract of a letter to T. J. Coleman, Esq., Banker, No. 63 Wall street.*]

CLEVELAND, Nov. 14, 1854.

Our friend Morrison, the banker, was burned out among the rest, but his safe stood the fire. I saw everything taken out of the safe, all in good order. It stood a tremendous fire, and it is said was red-hot a long time. It was one of Herring's safes.

Yours,

M. CRAPSER & CO.

ANOTHER SAFE IN SAME FIRE.

CLEVELAND, November 14, 1854.

S. C. Herring, Esq.:

SIR—On the 28th ult. our city was visited by the most disastrous fire that ever occurred in this place, destroying a large portion of the heavy business part of our great city. Our warehouse, containing a heavy stock of merchandise, was entirely consumed. The only valuables that we saved were contained in the safe purchased of you. Our books (a valuable set) and about $600 in money were recovered about twelve hours after the fire, and, we are happy to state, without the loss of a single dollar's worth. We shall be in your city in a few days and select another of your valuable safes.

L. F. & S. BURGESS.

LARGE FIRE AT CLEVELAND.

CLEVELAND, December 19, 1862.

Messrs. Herring & Co., New York:

GENTLEMEN—On the night of the 29th ultimo our establishment, with its contents, and some buildings adjoining were destroyed by fire. We owe the preservation of our books, valuable papers, and a large sum of money to the faithfulness of your Champion Safe. It was red-hot, yet brought forth its contents in excellent order; not a line was effaced or a dollar missing. We did not get the safe out until the building and contents were entirely destroyed. Send us another safe of a larger size immediately and we will return the old one.

It may be worth something for you to show its honored scars.

Yours respectfully,
A. STEPHENS & SONS.

ANOTHER LARGE FIRE IN CLEVELAND.

CLEVELAND, August 30, 1864.

Messrs. Herring & Co.:

GENTLEMEN—It gives me much pleasure to write you certifying to the fire-proof qualities of your justly celebrated safes, having had one in the building known as the "Old Baptist Church," when it was destroyed by fire on the night of the 6th of August.

The safe contained my books and valuable papers, which were preserved in excellent condition. The fire where the safe stood was very hot; and it was fortunate that I had it then in my possession.

WILLIAM GREEN.

FIRE AT MILAN.

MILAN, OHIO, November 17, 1849.

Mr. S. C. Herring:

DEAR SIR—A short time since our warehouse with several others was destroyed, and, being unable to get out the safe we purchased of you last spring, it was so badly roasted that the brass knob on the door was melted off and the outside of the safe very much sprung—so much so that we are afraid to trust it again to a like ordeal, should one occur—although it did us excellent service on that occasion, preserving our books and papers, not only so that they are perfectly legible, but in a condition that enables us to use them. We would inquire of you whether we can trust it again under like circumstances should they ever occur; and also how you will exchange for a new one of the same size and fashion.

Truly yours, STEVENS & RYAN.

Plate No. 31.

The FOUR INCH (four inches thick) Banker's Chests,

Made for BROWN, BROTHERS & CO.,

As they appear inside their vault.

FIRE AT REPUBLIC, APRIL, 1852.

[*From the Ohio Standard, July 1, 1852.*]

A day or two since we were invited to examine one of the above safes—the one owned by D. P. Russell, of Republic, and in his mill at the time it was burned on the 26th of April last. The mill was a large one (four stories high), and this safe was in the fire for *six hours*, after which it was dragged from the coals, suffered to cool, and then opened. The books and papers belonging to the mill were all in it, perfectly sound and whole, neither smoked nor sweated. This safe we think was *thoroughly tested ;* and those wishing to purchase a *fire-proof* article should procure one of Herring's Safes.

In consequence of the extreme heat and its falling from the second story its outward surface is much disfigured, but the shelving and drawers inside are as perfect as ever.

FIRE AT RAVENNA.

[*Extract from a letter.*]

RAVENNA, O., July 8, 1853.

Silas C. Herring :

SIR—Your letter of inquiry respecting the burning of our store and fate of safe duly came to hand. The fire was discovered in our three-story brick store about three o'clock in the morning. The safe was on the first floor, in the store-room, over some casks of linseed and lamp oil in the basement, and an attempt to remove the safe after our arrival at the fire was unsuccessful, as the wind was high and the fire burned with great rapidity, soon causing the floor, with the safe, to fall into the basement under the burning timbers and combustible materials of the upper stories. It remained in this situation until the fire subsided so that it could be reached with chains, and was then quite *red-hot ;* the outside plates warped and part of the wheels melted off. The safe contained bank-bills, books, notes, and papers to a large amount, which would have been an irretrievable loss to us had they been destroyed.

We supposed when the safe was removed from the fire, and the intense heat to which it had been so long exposed, that its contents must be destroyed ; but, upon opening it, to our surprise and satisfaction, we found the contents in a perfect state of preservation, except the binding of some of the books being a little discolored.

Respectfully yours,

S. A. & B. A. GILLETT.

FIRE AT PAINESVILLE.

PAINESVILLE, O., August 21, 1857.

Messrs. S. C. Herring & Co. :

GENTLEMEN—Our city was visited by a very destructive fire on the morning of the 4th instant, when a whole block of buildings was entirely consumed.

I fortunately was provided with one of your Herring's Safes, which stood the fire nobly, and, after removal from the ruins, looked nearly as well inside as when new.

C. S. BARTLETT.

P. S.—I shall call upon you and select a larger safe when I go to New York this fall. In the meantime I would like to have you send me a small one from your agent at Buffalo.

There was one of Lillie's safes in the same fire which was burned to ashes inside and broken in two.

MICHIGAN.

FIRE AT DETROIT, JUNE, 1849.

[From the Detroit Daily Advertiser.]

The following communication, from a business man of this city, addressed to the agent of Herring's Safes, may be relied upon as presenting facts which tend to establish and confirm the excellent character of this article, for the purpose for which it is intended. The ferry-house spoken of in the communication was a large building, and was entirely burned down.

DETROIT, MICH., June 24, 1849.

R. H. Hall, Agent for Herring's Safes:

DEAR SIR—It gives me great pleasure to inform you that the safe purchased of you by the late John Edwards was taken from the ruins of the fire on the night of the 15th inst., and, on opening it, found the contents perfect as when put in. The safe was on the second story of the ferry-house. It fell to the lower floor and was buried in the hottest of the fire. It being near the middle of the house, and in consequence of the great quantity of ruins heaped upon it, many hours elapsed before it could be got at. I think it a sufficient test of the superiority of your safes over all others.

THOS. GALLAGHER.

LARGE FIRE AT DETROIT.

DETROIT, MICH., Jan. 12, 1863.

Messrs. Herring & Co.:

GENTLEMEN—In these times, when so much is being said about fire-proof and burglar-proof safes, we deem it no more than our duty to put the community in possession of the facts connected with the test of one of your Champion Safes, and a test that should (if it has not already been done) settle the question as to where a certain and sure *Fire-proof* Safe can be obtained. We bought one of your No. 6 Safes from your agent in this city, B. Vernor. It was placed in the center of our frame store, at a point where three frame stores joined. On the night of January 7, 1863, the premises took fire, and the fire raged most furiously in the immediate vicinity of the safe. The fire made a most intense heat, from the large amount of combustible material in the immediate vicinity. So great was the heat that we made great efforts to have the safe removed, feeling that it might be too much risk to let it stay, if, by any means, it could be got out; but it was impossible, and the bystanders, among whom was a rival safe agent, assured us our case was a hopeless one, and we would find no contents when we got at the safe. After the fire, we, as soon as possible, got the safe out. It showed evidence of having been subjected to intense heat, and we opened it with great trepidation, and then, to our great relief, we found every item in good condition. We recommend Herring's Champion Safes most cheerfully to any one wanting a safe that is safe.

Yours truly,

PELGRIM, GRAY & CO.

GREAT FIRE IN DETROIT.

DETROIT, MICH., December 28, 1859.

B. Vernor, Agent for Herring's Patent Champion Safe:

DEAR SIR—We take great pleasure in informing you that one of your No. 5

Plate No. 32.

FOR DWELLINGS, &c.

No. 5—Toilet.   No. 5—Cabinet.

Inside.

20 in. high,
15 in. wide,
15 in. deep.

Boudoir.

No. 5½—Toilet.   No. 5½—Cabinet.

Inside Measure, 22 in. high, 17 in. wide, 15 in. deep.

Safes, owned by us, preserved its contents most effectually, and greatly to our satisfaction and that of the admiring crowd who witnessed its disinterment from the ruins of the four-story brick store occupied by us as a grocery and which was burned last night. The safe fell into the cellar and the timbers of all the floors fell and burned upon it, together with a ton of butter, and, after being exposed to this great test for nine hours, we opened it with perfect ease with the key. We most cheerfully recommend the Herring Champion Safe to any person in want of an article that is what it claims to be—a safe.

MILLER & JUDD.

GREAT FIRE AT MANCHESTER.

Manchester, Mich., July 26, 1854.

Silas C. Herring, Esq.:

Dear Sir—I have thought for some time past I would write to you to know if it would be safe to risk valuable books and papers in your safe after it had once been through a severe fire. One year ago my store was burned, and your safe, with my books and papers in it, was exposed to intense heat for several hours; in addition to the natural heat of the building, it received the flames from five tons of hams which hung under the counting-room. All the books came out perfectly safe. Some eighteen or twenty buildings were burned at the time, and I can give you as till a certificate as you could wish without telling anything but facts.

I see you have a Burglar and Powder-proof Lock, called Hall's Patent. Will you give me your prices with Hall's Patent Lock and oblige

Yours respectfully,
J. D. KIEF.

LARGE FIRE AT GRAND RAPIDS.

Grand Rapids, Mich., February 17, 1860.

Messrs. S. C. Herring & Co.:

Gentlemen— We had one of your No. 5 Safes in our law office, in the second story of the four-story brick building known as the Taylor & Barnes Block, in this city, which was destroyed by fire on the evening of the 23d of January, involving a loss of over $100,000.

The safe contained a large amount of valuable papers, our own and held in trust for others, involving a sum of at least $100,000, and fell into the cellar, where it lay in the midst of burning liquors, alcohol and other inflammable substances, causing the most intense heat, notwithstanding all of which, we are happy to say, it preserved its contents, thereby saving us an irreparable loss. We have this day bought another one, larger size, from your General Agent for Michigan, B. Vernor, and cheerfully recommend the Herring Champion Safe to every one.

ASHLEY & MILLER.

GREAT FIRE AT BUCHANAN.

Buchanan, Mich., November 7, 1862.

Messrs. Herring & Co., New York:

Gentlemen— Our store, which was a three-story and basement brick building, was totally destroyed by the recent large fire, which consumed most of the business portion of our town, on the 31st of October last. We had two of your Fire-proof Safes in use, which were subjected to an intense heat for twenty hours

One of them we have had eight years—its contents are as perfect as before the fire. The other we have had three years—it is one of your Herring's Patent Champions. The heat was so great around this safe that two of the iron wheels are partially melted off; yet the books and papers which it contained are as perfect as before the fire. We are now using the books and papers which both safes contained. The bindings of some of them are a little drawn by the steam from the fire-proof filling, which is the only indication that they have passed through a fire.

We have always had the utmost confidence in your Fire-proof Safes. The test has proved to us they are all you claim—perfect protection for books, papers, and so forth, from fire.

Yours respectfully,

ROSS, ALEXANDER & CO.

FIRE AT LOWELL.

LOWELL, MICH, January 6, 1862.

Messrs. Herring & Co., New York :

GENTLEMEN—On the morning of the 29th December our store was burned, together with all its contents. The store was a two-story wooden building, twenty-four by sixty-two feet, very strong and substantial.

Our books and papers were in one of your Patent Safes, which passed through the fire and preserved them completely.

The safe is somewhat damaged outside ; the panels are warped, and the temper of the lock must be drawn, for the safe was *red-hot*.

Will you take back the safe and sell us a new one? Our safe was bought by Mr. Hunt, April 16th, 1860, and cost $130. Please write us.

Yours truly,

HOOKER, HUNT & CO.

LARGE FIRE AT SAGINAW.

EAST SAGINAW, MICH., July 15, 1861.

Messrs. Herring & Co., New York :

GENTLEMEN—Our store and warehouse were totally consumed by fire on the morning of the 25th of June. We had one of your Patent Champion Safes in use. In it we had all of our books, papers, insurance policies, and some money, which were preserved. Not a line of writing, or leaf of our books, or any of the papers was injured in the least. The leather covers to the books were drawn by the steam. We had the books rebound, and are now using them the same as though nothing had happened. The fire was an extremely hot one, melting the brass ornamental plates and knobs on the doors completely off. The outside iron is much warped by the heat. We were unable to save anything from our stock of goods. Thanks to your safe, we have our books and papers preserved, which money could not replace.

Yours respectfully,

CURTIS, BLISS & CO.

P. S. It having been reported that our books and papers were destroyed by the late fire, we write the above to correct such rumors.

C., B. & CO.

GREAT FIRE AT DOWAGIAC.

DOWAGIAC, MICH., January 22, 1864.

Messrs. Herring & Co., Chicago :

GENTLEMEN—On the second of this month our village was visited with a severe fire, which burned the larger part of our business street, consisting of a block of eleven stores in which our store was located. We had one of your Herring's Patent Champion Safes, which was severely tested, it having fallen down on a pile of about three cords

Plate No. 33.

FOR DWELLINGS, &c.

No. 8—Toilet.

32 in. high,
22 in. wide, } Inside Measure.
15 in. deep,

No. 1—Sideboard Safe.

22 in. high,
28 in. wide, } Inside Measure.
16 in. deep,

of seasoned oak wood in the cellar and remained there until the building was entirely consumed. We found our books all safe, not injured with the exception of the leather binding of the books, which was melted by the steam from the fire-proof filling. I send you one of the books as a fair sample. I am surprised at the result of the safe after so severe a test, and now I want you to send me one of the same kind on your best terms.

Yours truly,
DANIEL LARZELERE.

FIRE AT JACKSON.

JACKSON, MICH., February 4, 1865.

Messrs. Herring & Co., Chicago, Ill. :

GENTLEMEN— In reply to yours of the 31st ult., we are glad to inform you that our books, papers, &c., contained in one of your Herring's Patent Champion Safes which was in our store at the time of its destruction by fire on the 28th of January last, were well preserved, except the binding of the books and the morocco note-case, which were damaged by the hot steam from the filling; otherwise they were all right.

We think the test has been a severe one for your safe. It stood on the lower floor of a three-story brick building (and no cellar), the two upper floors were heavily loaded, and when the joists were burned the two floors came down and covered all the lower floor and burned everything combustible. You can judge something of the intense heat the safe was subjected to.

Please send us a price-list and make us a proposition for exchange for a safe two or three sizes larger.

Yours truly,
RICE, GIBSON & PRATT.

ILLINOIS.

FIRES IN CHICAGO.

BURNING OF HADDOCK'S WAREHOUSE.

CHICAGO, ILL., November 15, 1851.

Mr. S. C. Herring :

SIR— In the recent destruction of my warehouse by fire, my safe (of your manufacture) was exposed for six hours to the most intense heat, and proved itself worthy of entire confidence in its ability to preserve its contents. My books and papers escaped *unsinged, even without discoloration ;* and the result is the more remarkable from the fact that a safe of another manufacture which was exposed at the same time was, with its contents, almost entirely destroyed.

Truly yours, &c.,
E. H. HADDOCK.

LARGE FIRE ON LAKE STREET.

[*Letter from Barnum Brothers.*]

CHICAGO, ILL., October 24, 1857.

C. L. Harmon & Co., Agents Herring's Safes, Chicago :

GENTLEMEN—The contents of Herring's Safe used by Messrs. Barnum Brothers in store No. 110 Lake street, Chicago, which has just been dug from the ruins of the great fire which occurred on the morning of Monday, 19th October instant, were found in a perfect state of preservation.

Yours,
R. F. BARNUM,
Surviving partner of Barnum Brothers.

BURNING OF BLATCHFORD'S LEAD WORKS.

CHICAGO, ILL., September 6, 1859.

C. L. Harmon & Co., Chicago, Agents Herring's Patent Champion Safe:

GENTLEMEN—During the disastrous conflagration of last night my lead pipe, sheet and bar lead manufactory, five stories in height and 55 by 100 feet on the ground, was completely destroyed and the walls nearly all fell. The Herring's Patent Champion Safe, size No. 2, high folding-doors, which Collins & Blatchford bought of you some three years since, was in my office on the second floor of the manufactory, and fell some twenty feet into the basement, where it lay exposed to a very severe heat for ten hours. Upon recovering it from the ruins to-day and opening it I found all my books, papers, and money contained in it in a good state of preservation—the only damage to them being the drawing of the leather binding of the books and their being quite damp from the safe being filled with steam from the fire-proof filling. The fire was of the most intense character, owing to the great height of the building and the fact that each story was in flames at once. I regard it as a most satisfactory test of the perfect fire-proof security afforded by Herring's Patent Champion Safe.

Yours truly,
E. W. BLATCHFORD.

BURNING OF FULLER & CO.'S WHOLESALE DRUG WAREHOUSE—FIFTY-EIGHT HOURS IN THE FIRE!!!

CHICAGO, ILL., November 4, 1860.

Messrs. Herring & Co.:

GENTLEMEN— It gives us great pleasure to inform you that the Herring's Patent Champion Safe purchased from you a few years ago has just passed through the fire which destroyed our store on the night of the 21st instant. Upon opening it we found all our books, papers, and money, in as good a state of preservation as when put in the safe, not a sign of fire on them, although it was not got out for fifty-eight hours after the fire commenced.

We can cheerfully recommend your safes as being all they claim to be—*the* Champion Safe of the world.

O. F. FULLER & CO.

DESTRUCTIVE FIRE AT POLO.

POLO, OGLE COUNTY. ILL., May 3, 1856.

C. L. Harmon & Co., Chicago, Agents for Herring's Champion Safes:

In October, 1855, I purchased of you a Herring's Patent Safe, No. 12,781. On the 22d of April, ult., my store was entirely consumed by fire, but the Safe proved equal to the test, and my books, papers, &c., came out entirely safe. The building was large, of wood, and filled with very combustible matter. The side of the building in which the safe stood was filled with alcohol, spirits of turpentine, and oil, rendering the heat excessively great—so great, in fact, as to melt down cast and wrought iron, such as stoves, nails, cast-iron kettles, &c., into an undistinguished mass. I had but little hope that the safe could stand so severe a test, but was happy to find it equal to the emergency.

Respectfully yours,
JAMES C. LUCKEY.

LARGE FIRE AT GENESEO.

BANKING-HOUSE OF NOURSE, BLAIR & CO.,
GENESEO, ILL., September 19, 1859.

Manufacturer of Herring's Safes:

DEAR SIR—This certifies that on the 6th day of February, 1859, our banking office was burned, and our safe, which was Herring's Patent, went through the fire and fell into the cellar, together with the burning timbers, where it remained many hours, until cool enough to be dragged out. Upon being opened the contents were found uninjured, and we now have the same safe in use. We recommend the Herring's Patent Champion to the public.

NOURSE, BLAIR & CO.

GREAT FIRE AT GALESBURG.

GALESBURG, ILL., June 26, 1861.

Messrs. Herring & Co.:

GENTLEMEN—It gives us much pleasure to inform you that in the late destructive fire in this place, the Herring's Patent Champion Safe which we purchased a few years since contained all our valuable books, papers, &c., which came out all right, and (with the exception of the binding of the books being curled by steam), in as good a state of preservation as when first put into the safe. We shall want another of larger size as soon as we get located.

Yours truly,
BARTLETT & JUDSON.

FIRE AT ST. CHARLES.

ST. CHARLES, ILL., September 30, 1861.

Messrs. Herring & Co.:

GENTLEMEN—This is to certify that, in the late destructive fire on the night of the 28th instant, which destroyed the three-story building in which my store was located, I had one of your Herring's Fire-proof Safes. The safe remained in the fire from 9 o'clock P. M. until 6 o'clock A. M., when the books, money, and papers were removed in good condition, and perfectly legible, so that I have no trouble in settling with my customers any more than if it had never been through a fire.

Respectfully yours,
J. P. FURNALD.

GREAT FIRE AT OTTAWA.

OTTAWA, January 23, 1866.

Messrs. Herring Co., New York:

GENTLEMEN—I received a letter from your house requesting me to let you know whether there were any of your safes in our last fire.

There was an old one of yours. It was in the second story, and as the building burned, fell through to the ground and lay there until the fire got low enough to pull it out. When it was cool enough the parties proceeded to open it, but finally concluded to cut the iron on the back and let the inside box out. They did so and found the steam and heat caused some papers to stick fast. But all came out safe.

The length of time the safe was in the fire I could not say exactly.

Yours truly,
DAVID SANDERSON.

INDIANA.

FIRE AT PLYMOUTH.

PLYMOUTH, IND., September 10, 1862.

Messrs. Herring & Co. :

GENTLEMEN—At the time of the very destructive fire which occurred here March 21, 1857, I had one of your fire-proof safes in use. I rolled it out in front of my store; the wind drove the flames directly upon it, only subjecting it to a blast or blow-pipe heat, which made the safe red-hot. Upon opening it, after it had become cooled, my books, papers, and money, which it contained, were perfectly preserved to my entire satisfaction.

Respectfully yours,

J. BROWNLEE.

BURNING OF FIRST NATIONAL BANK AT SOUTH BEND.

FIRST NATIONAL BANK,
SOUTH BEND, IND., May 24, 1865.

Messrs. Herring & Co., New York :

GENTLEMEN—On the night of the 25th ult. the building in which our bank was located (being a four-story building) was burned, and we were unable to get our safe out, so it went through the fire, there being some books, papers, and money, which all came out unburned.

Now, my object in writing is to ask if the safe had not better be refilled or repaired, in order to be safe in case of another fire. The safe is one of your make; hence I have taken the liberty of writing you on the subject. It is one of your large safes.

Very truly yours,

JOHN T. LINDSEY,
Cashier.

WISCONSIN.

GREAT FIRE AT MILWAUKEE.

MILWAUKEE, October 3, 1854.

Mr. S. C. Herring, New York :

SIR—Inclosed we hand certificates relating to your safes in the great fire in this city on the 24th August, which you are at liberty to publish.

Yours respectfully,

WILLIAMS, BONNELL & CO.,
Agents for Herring's Safes.

THE FIRST SAFE.

The first safe removed from the ruins was the property of Wm. E. Cramer, Esq., publisher and proprietor of the *Daily Wisconsin.* This safe was in the second story

Plate No. 34.

No. 8—Cabinet.

30 in. high,
24 in. wide,   Inside Measure.
15 in. deep,

Buffet Sideboard.

3 ft. 6½ in. high,
4 ft. 8 in. wide,   Outside.
2 ft. deep,

The heighth includes the wheels, which are 6 in. to 7 in.

of the Bank Buildings, and fell with the walls to the cellar. It was taken from the ruins twenty-six hours after the fire, with the contents in as good order as when put in.

ANOTHER.

Another safe, the property of Messrs. H. Bosworth & Sons, Druggists, fell with the floor to the cellar, and was surrounded with bricks and burning timbers twenty-eight hours, and when taken out the contents were in a good state of preservation —not a paper but was perfectly legible.

ANOTHER.

Another, the property of J. D. Gardiner, Esq., dry-goods merchant, was buried three feet under the falling ruins among heated bricks and timbers. This safe contained a large amount of notes and other papers, and some bank-bills, all of which came out in first-rate order.

ANOTHER.

Another, the property of Haney & De Bow, hardware merchants, remained in the ruins thirty hours. The mass of bricks which had fallen under, over, and round it, was hot enough to set wood on fire long after the safe had been removed. When this lay in the ruins the heat was so intense that different kinds of iron were melted into one mass. The contents of this were preserved, but slightly injured by steam, as an engine had to play upon it full an hour before opening it.

ANOTHER, AND TEST NO. 5.

Another, and Test Number Five, a safe belonging to George E. H. Day, Esq., was in the second story of Dickerman's Block and fell with the walls to the cellar; and for twenty hours after the fire was kept red-hot. The contents of this safe, when opened, were in the most perfect state of preservation.

ANOTHER, AND TEST NO. 6.

Another, and Test Number Six, was a No. 6 safe, belonging to Jason Downer, Esq., and was in the same building as the last (or No. 5), and fell to the cellar, where it remained thirty-six hours after the fire. The safe was brought to this city nine years ago by Wm. H. Hull, and was among the first ever made by Herring. The ordeal through which this safe passed was such that the iron on each side was partly melted off, but the contents were wholly uninjured.

TEST NO. 7.

Test Number Seven was a safe owned by Rood & Goodrich, jewelers, &c., and contained from $5,000 to $6,000 worth of jewelry, watches, and silver ware. It was located in the United States Hotel block. When opened, thirty-eight hours after the fire, everything—watches, earrings, silver spoons, &c.—was in good order, except a few pearl card-cases, a little tarnished by steam.

We, the undersigned, certify that the statements above, in relation to our respective safes, are true.

    WM. E. CRAMER,
    H. BOSWORTH & SONS,
    J. DOWNER,
    HANEY & DE BOW, } *Milwaukee, Wis.*
    J. D. GARDINER,
    ROOD & GOODRICH,
    GEO. E. H. DAY,

ANOTHER GREAT FIRE AT MILWAUKEE.

MILWAUKEE, January 22, 1861.

Lansing Bonnell, Agent for Herring's Safes :

DEAR SIR—In the recent fire which destroyed the Milwaukee city offices were two of Herring's safes, one large one in the City Clerk's office, located in the fourth story, and a smaller one in the School Commissioner's room in the third story.

We are happy to say, notwithstanding the safes fell so great a distance and were subjected to such an intense heat (the one forty and the other sixty hours), that the books and papers were in a first-rate state of preservation. The only injury received was the curling of the leather binding of the books by steam.

We think if the reputation of Herring's Safes was not fully established before this fire that all now must be satisfied that they are what they claim to be—fire-proof.

The castors on one and the plates on the other were melted off.

    FRANCIS HUEBSCHMANN, *Acting Mayor.*
    NELSON WEBSTER, *President Board of Councilors.*
    GEO. D. DOUSMAN, *City Clerk.*
    JONATHAN FORD, *Superintendent of Schools.*

THE GREAT FIRE AT OSHKOSH.

OSHKOSH, WIS., May 27, 1859.

Messrs. S. C. Herring & Co. :

GENTLEMEN—At the time of the recent large fire in the city of Oshkosh, which destroyed a large portion of the business street, the undersigned were each respectively the owners of Herring's Safe, and which were exposed to said fire, the buildings in which they were kept for use being entirely destroyed by said fire. We take pleasure in saying that the entire contents in each of our respective safes were wholly preserved, and realized our most sanguine expectations as to the fire-proof qualities of Herring's Safes.

    GABRIEL BOUCK,   C. PETERSLEA & CO.,
    WHEELER & COOLAUGH,   EIGHME, KENNEDY & HANCOCK,
    L. H. COTTRILL.   G. W. WASHBURN.
    S. B. & S. A. PAIGE,

OSHKOSH, WIS., May 20, 1859.

Messrs. S. C. Herring & Co. :

GENTLEMEN—On the night of the 10th instant, during the great conflagration which destroyed a large portion of our city, our store was entirely consumed ; but, fortunately, our books, papers, and considerable sums of money in bank-bills were in one of your Champion Safes, and, on opening it, we found them all per-feet and uninjured, after having been in the ruins fifteen hours in a heat that melted off the plates, &c., from the doors.

Yours, &c.,

K. M. HUTCHINSON.

BANK OF OSHKOSH.

Oshkosh, Wis., May 28, 1859.

At the time of the late fire in our city we had in our bank two of your safes of different sizes. The larger one we purchased in Buffalo for $375; the other cost $150. (We mention the cost that you may judge of the size.) These safes were both removed from the building before the fire reached us. The small safe was moved across the walk, eight feet from the building, and received little or no injury. The contents were perfect as when put in. The larger safe, being difficult to handle, was got out through the side of the building, falling upon the sidewalk, with the lower end of the safe probably within one foot of the building, where it was allowed to remain to the next A.M. THE WIND DROVE THE FLAMES CONTINUALLY ON THIS SAFE while our building was burning. I am not satisfied in my own mind whether we INCREASED OR DIMINISHED the exposure of our large safe by moving it from the building and leaving it where we did. Nothing in the safe was destroyed. The leather-bound books we have got rebound, and continue to use them, they being now as good as before the fire. Everything in the safe was quite damp; but, as I said before, NOTHING WAS DESTROYED.

Respectfully,

ANSEL W. KELLOGG,
Cashier.

LARGE FIRE AT WAUPON.

Waupon, Wis., August 24, 1857.

Mr. Lansing Bonneil, Agent for Herring's Safes:

DEAR SIR—The Herring's Champion Safe that I purchased of you was in my store at the time it was burned last March. The heat was so great that it melted off the brass plates and knob on the front of the safe. The door was warped so badly from heat that I was obliged to cut it open. But I am happy to say to you the contents of the safe were preserved to my *perfect satisfaction.*

Yours, &c.,

Y. C. SNOW.

FIRE IN BERLIN.

OFFICE OF REESE & WILLIAMS,
Wholesale and Retail Grocers,
Berlin, Wis., March 30, 1861.

Messrs. Herring & Co., Chicago:

GENTLEMEN—Yours of the 25th instant is at hand. In regard to the safes that passed through our late fire, we would reply that there were but two in the fire. One of your make was in the hottest part of the ruins and saved all its contents, about $3,000 in money and valuables, belonging to the *American Express Company.* The other was an old safe; it bore no maker's name; it was badly used up; the books and papers inside were a little charred on the edges and covers.

The Herring Safe is one of the smallest in size that is made, and was owned by D. H. Carhart, Agent American Express Company.

Yours, &c.,

REESE & WILLIAMS.

FIRE IN EAST TROY.

EAST TROY, WIS., April 9, 1853.

Mr. S. C. Herring:

SIR—Some years since I purchased of you one of your safes. In March I was so unfortunate as to have my store burned; but, through the instrumentality of your safe, my books and papers were preserved, and I feel proud to say that not a word or even a letter was defaced, or in any manner rendered unintelligible. I wish to procure another of the same kind as I shall never feel secure without one of your safes, and wish you to forward me one of your size No. 2, with box, at about $240.

E. H. BALL.

FIRE IN PORTAGE CITY.

PORTAGE CITY, WIS., September 26, 1861.

Messrs. Herring & Co.:

GENTLEMEN—Our iron foundry and machine shop were totally destroyed by fire on the morning of August 21. We were using one of your Patent Champion Safes. After hauling it from the ruins and giving it time to cool we endeavored to unlock it, but the heat had disarranged the lock, and the door was so much warped we were compelled to break it open. Our books, notes, valuable papers, and money were entirely preserved; the only injury done was the removal of the leather covers of the books, which, we are informed, was done by the steam from the fire-proof composition. The fire was a very hot one, as the exterior of the safe shows, the brass ornamental plates and knob of the lock having been melted off. Some of our iron was melted and run into flakes as it would have been in a furnace. When a safe proves, as this one has, its claim to the title of fire-proof, we believe full justice should be done to the manufacturers.

Yours respectfully,

DEAN & SMITH.

GREAT FIRE AT RACINE.

RACINE, WIS., January 29, 1866.

Messrs. Herring & Co., 40 State street, Chicago, Ill.:

GENTLEMEN—In the late destructive fire in this city I had one of your Herring's Patent Champion Safes of the smallest size, which was exposed to a very severe heat and came out all right, preserving my books and papers in as good shape as I would wish. There were two "Fire King" safes of larger size, which were not so much exposed, but were very badly scorched and not to be compared with mine.

Please send me the safe at which I looked when in your store last week.

Signed,

F. HUBACHEK.

IOWA.

FIRE AT DUBUQUE.

DUBUQUE, IOWA, January 7, 1859.

Messrs. S. C. Herring & Co.:

GENTLEMEN—I am requested by Mr. T. A. C. Cochrane, of this place, to say to

Plate No. 35.

Parlor Safe.

26 in. high,
21 in. wide, Inside Measure.
15 in. deep,

Sideboard Silver Chest

31 in. high,
17 in. wide, Inside Measure.
17 in. deep,

you that on the morning of the 4th instant, about 3 o'clock, his store took fire and the entire stock of goods was destroyed. The heat became so suddenly intense that none of the goods could possibly be saved; but, fortunately, his books and papers, which were in one of your Champion Safes, were all preserved perfectly. And well they may be called Champion, for during the whole conflagration there was one incessant pouring of flame directly upon the safe which contained them. And still, upon opening it, the inside was found to be scarcely warm, while the outside was severely scorched.

Yours truly,   N. A. McCLURE.

FIRE IN IOWA.

UNITED STATES LAND OFFICE,
DUBUQUE, IOWA, May 28, 1859.

Messrs. S. C. Herring & Co., New York:

GENTLEMEN—The Champion Safe which I purchased of you last season through N. A. McClure, Esq., your agent in this city, has just passed through as severe a test as any safe will probably ever be subjected to in any conflagration. It was in the center of my office, on the second floor of the "Old Fellows' Hall" building in this place, which was totally consumed night before last, and was exposed for a long time to the most intense heat, dropping finally into the cellar, where it was buried by the falling walls without being broken or crushed. Yesterday it was exhumed, still very hot, and I felt great anxiety to know its condition, containing, as it did, money to the amount of several hundred dollars, mostly in bank-notes, land warrants worth several thousand dollars, besides notes of hand and other valuable papers and books. This morning it was opened and, to my great satisfaction, all the papers, &c., were found uninjured and perfect in every respect. I heartily congratulate you, as the manufacturers, and myself, as the possessor, of that which may be truly and emphatically called a safe.

Very respectfully your obedient servant,

ALEX. D. ANDERSON,
Register.

FIRE AT DAVENPORT.

DAVENPORT, IOWA, July 29, 1862.

Messrs. Herring & Co., Chicago:

GENTLEMEN I am the owner of a safe manufactured by you. Said safe was in a Grain Elevator in this place, and which Elevator was burned some two months since. The safe came out in fine condition, the money and papers in a good state of preservation. The fire was one of the largest that ever occurred here and one of intense heat. We had to cut the door open (the lock being injured by the heat).

Yours, &c.,   J. C. WASHBURN.

MINNESOTA.

GREAT FIRE IN WINONA,

EXTENDING OVER TEN ACRES AND NEARLY DESTROYING THE TOWN.

WINONA COUNTY BANK,
WINONA, MINN., July 26, 1862.

Messrs. Herring & Co., Chicago:

GENTLEMEN—We had one of your large size Herring's Patent Safes in the great fire of July 5, 1862, and our books and papers came out uninjured except the covers and binding of the books.

Respectfully yours,

WEBSTER & LAKE.

ANOTHER.

WINONA, July 12, 1862.

Messrs. Herring & Co., Chicago:

GENTLEMEN—I had one of your Fire-proof Safes in the large fire which took place here on the night of the 4th inst. It faithfully preserved its contents, consisting of books, papers, and jewelry. My soft solder goods even were not injured. I shall require another safe as soon as my new place is ready.

Yours respectfully,

GEO. L. BROWN, *Jeweler*.

KANSAS.

BURNING AND BOMBARDMENT OF OSSAWATOMIE.

OSSAWATOMIE, KANSAS, December 20, 1856.

S. C. Herring & Co.:

GENTLEMEN—On the 30th of August last my office at this place, containing the Herring's Patent Champion Safe, purchased of you last winter, was attacked and burned by the Missouri Army, under Captain Reid.

After the fire they attacked the safe and fired two cannon balls against it without effect, and I am pleased to say that the safe withstood the fire and the bombardment, and I have it now in use.

Yours truly,

O. C. BROWN.

BURNING OF THE CITY OF LAWRENCE.

LAWRENCE, KANSAS, September 18th, 1856.

Messrs. Herring & Co.:

GENTLEMEN—In answer to your inquiries we are happy to say that the safe we had in use at the time our city was destroyed and sacked by the rebels, August 21st, 1863, was a Herring's Patent Champion made by you. In the plundering of the town before the fire was started, the raiders entered our store and made a desperate attempt to force the safe with hammers, chisels, &c., breaking off the hinges. But all was vain; the safe resisted the attempt to rob, and was afterward, in the burning of the city, exposed to the hottest kind of fire. It is with confidence we state what has been acknowledged by all here who saw the safe and its contents after it was taken from the ruins, that no safe in the burnt district was subject to more heat, if as much, as this was. The building which we occupied was framed of heavy oak timber, and the large quantity of agricultural implements we had on hand created a heat of the most intense character. The safe was found in the ruins after two days' roasting, but everything it contained—books, papers, and money—was preserved in first-rate order, no injury whatever, except the cracking or steaming of the backs of the books.

Yours respectfully,

A. STORM & CO.

COLORADO.

THE GREAT FIRE AT DENVER CITY.

DENVER CITY, COL., April 21, 1863.

Messrs. Herring & Co., Chicago:

GENTLEMEN—On the 19th inst. a large fire occurred at this place, destroying a large amount of property. We had one of your safes in our store at that time, which was surrounded by about 500 gallons of coal oil, also a large amount of varnishes, turpentine, rosin, &c., which made a fearful fire. Our building and stock were entirely lost. All that we saved were our books and papers that were in the safe. When we opened it we found the contents in good condition, and the safe looks as if it would stand another just such a fire.

Yours respectfully,

E. T. CHEESMAN & CO.

P. S.—Please send us another No. 5 Safe immediately, as we have sold our old one.

ANOTHER.

DENVER CITY, COL., April 21, 1863.

Messrs. Herring & Co., Chicago:

GENTLEMEN—We take pleasure in informing you that, in the destructive fire which took place here on the 19th inst., our safe (one of your Herring's make) preserved all our books and papers and quite a large sum of money in a perfectly satisfactory manner, so that we are now using all of the same.

There were some safes here of other makers in the same fire which did not turn out so well. We shall want another of your safes soon.

Yours truly,

COOKE & BRO.

CALIFORNIA.

GREAT FIRE AT SAN FRANCISCO, MAY 4, 1850.

[*From the New York Tribune, June, 1850.*]

THE SALAMANDER SAFE IN CALIFORNIA.—Mr. Silas C. Herring, the celebrated maker of the Salamander Safe, has received from California an interesting description of the late destructive conflagration at San Francisco and of the unequaled virtues of the "Salamanders" on the occasion in a letter written, after a visit to the ruins, by Jacob L. Dodge, Esq., late Alderman of the Ninth Ward of this city and now a resident of California. Mr. Dodge says: "After the fire was over I walked over the ruins and found everything in ashes, except here and there a *Salamander Safe*. There was not one of these which, when opened, did not turn out everything in as perfect order as when first put in. Some of them contained over $200,000 in gold dust, besides valuable papers, and one of them contained two gold watches, which came out *in running order, marking the exact time!* Not only had the watches continued to run, but the other contents of these safes were entirely uninjured. This is justly considered wonderful among the San Franciscans." The watches alluded to had been in the fire some twelve hours, during eight of which the safes were surrounded by red-hot coals. Mr. Dodge adds that having made some remarks commendatory of the Salamanders (judging of their virtues from his own previous experience), a bystander ridiculed the eulogiums he had passed upon them, offering at the same time a wager of a thousand dollars that everything in the safe in question was destroyed. Feeling so well assured (continues Mr. D.) from what I had seen and know of the quality of the Salamander of my old friend Herring, I immediately turned to take the gentleman at his word; but he now declined, being probably convinced from my manner that he was in the wrong. In the meantime the safe had been taken from the ruins, and the examination immediately instituted showed that not an article contained in it was scorched. The result of the examination was received with three cheers by about five hundred spectators. Mr. Dodge adds that there were from eighty to one hundred iron safes (so called) in the fire, of which from twenty-five to thirty were of Mr. Herring's manufacture. All but the Salamanders were burned to ashes with their contents.

This new test of the serviceable qualities of the Salamander Safe will give general satisfaction to those who have already experienced the benefits of this invention. A reputation has been established for them in the Gold Regions second only to that which they have so long enjoyed elsewhere.

The *Alta California*, in its account of the fire of the 4th of May at San Francisco, having spoken disrespectfully of the "Salamanders," made the following handsome retraction.

[*From the Daily Alta California.*]

SAN FRANCISCO, May 7, 1850.

SAFES.—In the use of the word "Salamander," in an article touching Safes in yesterday's *Alta*, we did not intend it to apply to Herring's. We make this statement because we are informed that such a construction was erroneously placed upon the language. The word, as we used it, was a mere "figure of speech."

SAN FRANCISCO, CAL., May 24, 1850.

Silas C. Herring, Esq., New York:

DEAR SIR—We have great pleasure in informing you (likewise we consider it a duty due to the public) that we had in use two of your safes in our building known as the "Empire," opposite Portsmouth square, fronting on Kearney street, during the late calamitous fire of the 4th instant, the particulars of which disaster will reach your city by mail per steamer Isthmus.

The houses adjacent to the Empire were large; and being constructed of wood, and the large quantity of combustible material contained in them, we entertained fears in regard to the safety of the safes. Notwithstanding the ravages of the fire, they remained in the ruins, in consequence of the intense heat, about twelve hours before they could be removed. The largest contained gold and silver coin to the amount of $200,000, and the smaller one, packages of gold dust and sundry valuable papers. The coin was in no manner injured, nor even the papers scorched; all were in perfect order.

Under these trying circumstances and the great calamity that our city has experienced, we really feel grateful that we were in possession of two of your good and now thoroughly tested safes, which we consider are well worthy the attention and confidence of all.

Respectfully yours,

BUCKLIN & BOOKSTAVER.

Plate No. 36.

Buffet Sideboard Safe, with top.

Inside.	Outside.
28 in. high,	3 ft. 6 in. high,
60 in. wide,	6 ft. wide,
14 in. deep.	2 ft. deep.

HERRING'S FIRE-PROOF SAFES.

SAN FRANCISCO, CAL., May 14, 1850.

Silas C. Herring, Esq., New York:

In conversation with our mutual friend, Mr. Jacob L. Dodge, formerly of your city, the worthless condition of the so-called "Fire-proof Safes," which were destroyed in the fire of the 4th instant caused us, in company with him, to make a thorough examination of them; and we found that, with the exception of your safes, they were perfectly worthless. We deem it but justice to you and to the public to make these facts known, and would say that you are at perfect liberty to publish this or use it in any way you think proper.

With much respect, we are yours, &c.,

PAYNE & SHERWOOD,
Auctioneers and Commission Merchants, 247 Montgomery street.

GREAT FIRE IN SAN FRANCISCO.

SAN FRANCISCO CITY, CAL.

Mr. Silas C. Herring:

SIR—About two years since I purchased from you one of your safes, and in the great fire in this city, on the 4th of May, when our city was nearly destroyed, that safe was in my store and exposed to the fury of the flames, and was not recovered from the ruins for some days. It was on the first floor, and there were about 300 boxes of tin-plate in the same room. So hot was the fire that the tin-plate was partially melted, and each box became a solid mass of metal. Yet, strange as it may appear, all the books, papers and money—in fact, everything that was in the safe, came out uninjured. I now require one of larger size, and consider them the best insurance, at the smallest premium, for every one that has papers of value to protect from fire.

JAMES DE LA MONTANYA.

FIRE AT SACRAMENTO CITY.

SACRAMENTO CITY, CAL., Tuesday, August 15, 1854.

Silas C. Herring, Esq.:

SIR—Early in 1852 we purchased at your store, No. 139 Water street, New York, one of your Patent Safes, and had some of our valuables and papers preserved in it during the great fire of November 2, 1852; and that, though the safe stood in the second story of the building and fell through into the cellar, and remained there eight days among the burning ruins of one of the largest stocks of liquors and provisions in this city (viz., Messrs. Meeker & Co.'s), and having thus acquired unlimited confidence in its ability to protect its contents unharmed from any conflagration, we, accordingly, upon the breaking out of the fire of July 13, 1854, filled it with such of our books, papers, and other articles of value as were in our office—such as deeds, mortgages, notes, dental instruments, and daguerrean likenesses—and it proved true to its trust again, for it took its contents through the second fiery ordeal unharmed and uninjured.

Feeling grateful for its former services, we have had it painted up, and should we be again so unfortunate as to need its services, will trust to it implicitly and unhesitatingly. We write this supposing you have never heard of these incidents, and thinking the maker of such safes is entitled to a certificate of their good qualities.

Respectfully yours,

BOYD & DAVIS.

GREAT FIRE IN STOCKTON.

STOCKTON, CAL., June 12, 1865.

Mr. S. C. Herring, New York:

DEAR SIR—We have now and have had for some time in our possession, in continual use, one of your safes. This safe has been through three large fires; the last one of which used it pretty roughly—melted one leg into a round, rough chuck clean off. But not a paper was hurt, and books and notes came out perfectly clean and unhurt each time. We now use the safe for all our business, and consider it as safe as ever; but it looks ugly, and we have thought that it would be the best advertisement in the world for you to have it standing in front of your office or manufactory, with the necessary affidavits from here what fires it has gone through and how well it stood the test.

We remain, respectfully yours,
HOBE & WEIHE.

CANADA.

FIRE IN COLBORNE, MARCH 26, 1852.

COLBORNE, CANADA WEST, April 5, 1852.

Silas C. Herring, Esq., New York:

DEAR SIR — Having had the misfortune to have my building burned, 26th March last, in which I had one of your safes, which was exposed to the most intense heat, so much so that the stoves melted; and after removing the brick and getting the safe from the ruins, I found the temper out of the springs of the locks and some of the plate broken by the falling of the walls. Therefore, I have shipped it to you for repairs or to send me a new one in exchange. When it arrives, please write me what you can do with it in the shape of repairs, or how you will exchange and give another for it, the same size. I have none at present, and would like to have one as soon as possible. I trust you will take into consideration that I was not covered by any insurance, and feel the want of another at as good terms as possible. Waiting your favors,

I am your obedient servant,
J. D. HAYES.

ANOTHER FIRE AT COLBORNE, CANADA WEST.

COLBORNE, September 15, 1854.

Mr. S. C. Herring:

Mr. Wood's store in this place was last night consumed by fire, in which was the safe had of you containing all our books, papers, and money, and it was subjected to the most intense heat, so much so as to melt the hinges of the doors, and a keg of nails standing near was melted and ran into one solid mass. A smoke or hot steam was seen issuing out of the safe, and all supposed it was the burning books. When the safe was taken out of the ruins, a crowd gathered round to see it opened, all expecting to see nothing but cinders; but, to their astonishment, every book and paper, and the money, came out perfect, as far as the paper and writing was concerned; the steam had softened the glue of the covers; but everything else was as good as new. I shall be in New York in a few days and get another. This is the second one of your safes that has been burned in the same building, both of which have proved true, and justly entitle your safes to be called the Champion.

Yours,
J. D. HAYES.

Plate No. 37.

Vault Doors.

6 ft. high, } in clear of door.
2 ft. wide, }

Express Messenger Box.

THE GREAT FIRE AT MONTREAL.

[*Extract from a letter dated Montreal, June 9th, 1852.*]

Silas C. Herring :

I send you two papers, by which you will see that we have been visited with a great conflagration, attended with a great loss of property ; most, however, was insured. One of your safes, belonging to the " Harbor Commissioners," was exposed to a most severe trial, being in the second story of a building over a ship-chandler's store, filled with rosin, pitch, tar, and other materials of the same nature ; and, in addition to this, the flames of eight or ten buildings were blowing in the direction of the safe, making, perhaps, one of the hottest fires that a Salamander was ever exposed to. It fell about thirty feet to the cellar, where it lay buried in the burning ruins about thirty hours over a hot fire. It was opened yesterday in the presence of several merchants and others, who were surprised to find the papers and bank bills all O. K. This test has proved the fire-proof quality of your safes in this section of the country. The lock had to be broken, and the safe is useless, except as a specimen of security to all who want a good safe.

Yours in haste,
GEO. HAGAR.

ANOTHER LARGE FIRE AT MONTREAL.

[*From the Montreal Herald, April 28, 1864.*]

DESTRUCTIVE FIRE AND LOSS OF LIFE.—About nine o'clock yesterday morning a fire occurred in St. Nicholas street, by which the extensive paint and oil warehouses of Messrs. E. Atwater & Co. was entirely destroyed.   *

When the safe was recovered, it was opened by the aid of a locksmith, and the books, papers, and a quantity of money were found perfectly safe. The safe was one of HERRING'S PATENT.

MONTREAL, April 27, 1864.

Messrs. Herring & Co., New York :

At the great fire this morning, at Messrs. E. Atwater & Co.'s paint, oil, and varnish store, one of Herring's Patent Safes was exposed to a severe trial ; but, on opening the safe, the books, papers, and money were found all safe as usual.

GEORGE HAGAR.

FIRE AT MOUNT BRIDGES.

MOUNT BRIDGES, July 4, 1855.

F. B. Beddome, Esq., London, C. W., Agent for Herring & Co.:

DEAR SIR—I am sorry to inform you that my store, with the whole of the contents, furniture, clothing, &c., was destroyed by fire last night. I saved nothing. You will remember I bought one of Herring's Safes from you last March, and I have much pleasure in informing you it stood the fire well ; it was perfectly red hot for several hours. The handles and brass plate both melted off and after hanging it out of the burning embers we had to pour water on it for nearly half an hour before it could be opened. You may fancy my satisfaction at finding my books mortgages, deeds, notes, and cash all right. I had a large amount of valuable papers in it, which, had I lost, would have completely ruined me. You will please send me another safe directly, and I will send you the old one, that you may show it to all who may wish to have a perfectly fire-proof safe.

I remain, dear sir, yours respectfully,

J. W. EMERSON.

FIRE IN LONDON.

LONDON, C. W., April 17, 1863.

SIR—We had the misfortune, on the 28th of December last, to have our store burned; but were very fortunate in having one of your Champion Safes, which preserved our books and papers entire, free from injury.

The fire was intensely hot, and it was supposed impossible for any safe to resist the heat; but our books were as completely preserved as if they had not been in any fire.

THOMAS FORBES & CO.

HERRING'S SAFES
IN FOREIGN COUNTRIES.

FIRE AT ST. THOMAS, W. I.

NEW YORK, May 27, 1856.

S. C. Herring & Co.:

GENTLEMEN—Some four or five years since I purchased of you one of your Fire-proof Safes for my store in St. Thomas, which was burned in March, 1855, and I am happy to say my books and papers were preserved in the safe without material injury. I shall feel secure as long as I have one of your safes.

JOSEPH RIDGWAY,
Then of the firm of Whitmore & Co.

GREAT FIRE IN JAPAN.

DESTRUCTION OF A LARGE AMOUNT OF AMERICAN PROPERTY—JAPANESE ENGINES—HERRING'S SAFES—SINGULAR PLAN TO CHECK A FIRE—A FOREIGN FIRE BRIGADE, ETC., ETC.

[*Correspondence of the Boston Traveller.*]

NAGASAKI, JAPAN, January 6, 1860.

On the morning of the 26th of December, the foreigners of Nagasaki awoke to find the places of two of our most prominent merchants burned to the ground—one being the premises of the American Consul at this port, comprising his offices, godowns, and storehouses; the other the property of Messrs. David Sassoon, Son & Co. (a prominent Parsee house), comprising their storehouses, godowns, and the private residence of their partner here, Mr. Ezekiel. The American Consulate happily escaped, being in another part of the town.

The fire commenced near the premises of Messrs. Sassoon, and soon extended to their place—their building being all of wood and as combustible as possible. Their place being situated next to Mr. F. G. Walsh's (the American Consul), soon inclosed his in flames. The fire broke out about two o'clock A. M., on the 26th instant, in an unoccupied Japanese house, and was, without doubt, the work of an incendiary, (the punishment for which, in this country, is to be burned alive). The property lost is estimated to be about $150,000 by F. G. Walsh, and $250,000 by Messrs. Sassoon & Co.

At seven o'clock A. M. every thing was burned to the ground. The Governor and suite were present, and also any quantity of Japanese; the wooden engines, with a single action, throwing water by jerks about thirty feet. Also, a number of Japanese with huge fans, placed on the adjoining houses and fanning the fire to keep it away. The fire dresses of the officials, of which there were some thousands upon the ground, were of the utmost magnificence, and the whole scene of the flames, and the brilliant and splendid clothing of the Japanese, formed a picture that must be witnessed to be appreciated.

The safe of the American Consul (one of Herring's, New York) came out of the flames all right, with the exception of the lock being out of order, and it had to be broken open.

All foreigners are now about to form themselves into a fire brigade, and to be prepared with axes, &c., to be ready in case of fire to assist one another.

[*Extract from the Straits Times of February 4, 1860, published at Singapore.*]

The American Consul's safe is all right. One of Herring's, New York, came out of the flames in fine order, although put to a severe test.

GREAT FIRE AT BARBADOES.

BARBADOES, W. I., April 26, 1860.

Messrs. S. C. Herring & Co., No. 251 Broadway, New York:

GENTLEMEN—We forward by this vessel (the Icarion) one of your Patent Champion Fire-proof Safes, which we imported through your consul here, the late Mr. Noble Towner, some eighteen months since. This safe was in our establishment during the *awful fire* of the 14th February last, and remained there more than forty-eight hours, until the whole building was totally consumed. An immense heat, coming from our own stores, as well as from a coal-yard with over three hundred tons of coal, situated about twenty feet to windward of that part of the building in which the safe was kept, rendered it impossible for any one to approach the ruins at an earlier period. The safe contained jewelry as well as the book which we send along with this. On opening the safe we found (as per certificate on the book, to which we ask reference) that the jewelry was only slightly tarnished and will be easily repolished. The book will show you the value of the safes for protecting papers, &c. Your consul was present at the opening of the safe, and it is at his request we send it to you. His regretted death since this occasion precludes us from having his signature to the certificate. You can keep the safe to show your customers, and ship us another of the same size. You may retain the book and certificate and make any use you like of them.

We remain yours truly,

BARROW & DUMMETT.

BOMBARDMENT OF GREYTOWN.

NEW YORK, October 25, 1854.

S. C. Herring, 135 Water street:

SIR—I was a resident at Greytown at the time of its destruction by fire in July last, when four buildings belonging to me, together with the whole town, were consumed, and very little of value was saved, except the contents of two of your safes; one of them belonged to the Saranac House, and the other to Messrs. De Forrest & Co., both of which, after the fire, were opened in the presence of myself and many others, and the books and papers were taken out uninjured.

I am yours respectfully,

BENJAMIN MOONEY.

PORTO RICO.

THE GREAT FIRE IN MAYAGUEZ.

MAYAGUEZ, April, 1862.

Messrs. Herring & Co.:

GENTLEMEN—At the great fire in this place on the 11th March we had in use one of your Patent Fire-proof Safes.

The safe remained in the fire until the following day, when we had it removed and opened. We are pleased to inform you that the interior of the safe and the papers which were in it were in excellent condition and uninjured by the fire.

MICHELENA & CO.

BURGLAR-PROOF.

We are often asked the question—Are these safes burglar-proof? and invariably answer they are as much protection against the burglar as the price paid will admit. This is the most that can be said for any safe. Nothing is made by man that man cannot unmake; and a safe made for books and papers only as a fire-proof protection is not a fit receptacle for coupon bonds, government securities, or large amounts of money.

The situation of a safe, the chances that burglars may have to work upon it undisturbed, the amount in money, bonds, or other valuable property that the burglar could realize on, are all important elements in its security against force or all the means that rogues can bring to bear. Within a few years back—in fact, since the great influx of paper money and securities—the highest amount of ingenuity and talent to be found among the burglar fraternity has been stimulated and developed by the ease with which these securities are converted into money, so that it is now universally admitted that burglar-proof means protection for a certain length of time against such tools and means as a burglar can bring to bear; that is, a safe may resist for one hour or for ten hours, just in proportion to its strength. But when our customers want protection for large sums, they must pay for more work, more labor, and more thickness of metal, and they can have just as strong a safe as they choose to pay for.

Our BANK SAFES and BANK VAULT DOORS are made of a combination of wrought iron, steel bars, and HERRING & FLOYD'S NEW PATENT CRYSTALLIZED IRON—the only metal now known which cannot be drilled by a burglar.

The experiments and tests recently made with the patent crystallized iron have fully demonstrated its superiority to hardened steel, or chilled iron, as a drill-resistant, the peculiar formation of the grain of the iron being such that it will completely cut or grind off the point and edges of a drill.

Our Burglar-proof Safes, and also our Fire and Burglar-proof Safes combined, are made with great care, finished in the best manner, and we believe them to be the most complete and perfect protection now in the market. For a full description of their construction the public are referred to our "BANKERS' PAMPHLET."

Our COMBINED FIRE AND BURGLAR, or BANKERS' SAFE is constructed by making two complete safes and placing *one within* the other—the outer safe is to protect from fire, the inside from burglars. This gives the purchaser double advantage. Against fire it is more secure, as the mass of metal comprising the burglar safe is put *inside* of the fire-proof lining (in place of outside, the ordinary way), and consequently removed from proximity to the fire, and cannot absorb and retain the heat as though exposed on the outside. Against burglars it is also much more effective, as there are two safes to get into, and the inside safe can never be operated on with the same facility that one could be outside.

The inner chest is made from two to four inches thick, at the option of the purchaser, of wrought iron, steel bars, and the new metal, SPIEGEL-EISEN, or Patent Crystallized Iron—the best protection against drilling or cutting tools yet discovered. These chests are also furnished with combination locks without key or keyhole. The locks vary in price from $75 to $300.

DWELLING-HOUSE SAFES,

For Silver Plate, Valuable Papers, Ladies' Jewelry, &c., &c.

The subscribers pay particular attention to the manufacture of safes for *Private Residences*, and have a large assortment constantly on hand, at prices varying from $100 to $1,500. These safes are grained—oak, walnut, rosewood, mahogany, or any color preferred—to imitate furniture, at the desire of the purchaser.

SIDEBOARD and PARLOR SAFES of elegant workmanship and finish, with marble tops, &c., made to resemble a handsome piece of furniture. Drawings of these safes, with their prices, will be given upon application.

Plate No. 38.

Bank Vault Doors.

6 ft. 6 in. high, }
2 ft. 4 in. wide, } In clear of door.

Outer door 2¼ in. thick, a combination of Wrought Iron, Steel Bars
and SPIEGEL EISEN.

OVER 30,000 HERRING'S FIRE-PROOF SAFES

have been made and sold, and are now in use in every State and Territory of this country and among more than thirty different foreign nations.

At the World's Fair, London, 1851, they were awarded the Prize Medal, as the best safe made in the world; also at the Crystal Palace, New York, 1853, they carried off the first prize.

They have been similarly honored by the State Fairs of New York, Pennsylvania, Michigan, Virginia, Missouri; also by the American Institute, New York; the Franklin Institute, Philadelphia; the Metropolitan Institute, Washington city. And wherever they have been placed for competition they have been universally acknowledged to be the best article of the kind ever manufactured.

THE GREAT ATTEMPTED BANK ROBBERY AT THE NEW YORK EXCHANGE BANK.

Herring's Safe foils the burglars and saves $500,000.

NEW YORK, March 27, 1861.

Messrs. Herring & Co., No. 251 Broadway:

GENTLEMEN—You have already been well informed through the columns of the daily papers of the desperate attempt made upon our money vault and the fire and burglar-proof safe made by you for our bank a few years ago. Although our vault was very strongly built and provided with heavy doors and the best of locks, the attempt upon the vault was successful.

The rogues succeeded in undermining the vault by digging a tunnel some seventy feet long under the adjoining building and terminating at the base of the vault itself. Here they commenced their operations upon a large scale, and, after removing the front part of the heavy stone foundation, which was strongly laid in cement, they reached the large flag-stone which formed the floor of the vault. This stone was broken by means of a Jack-screw of great power, and the interior of the vault thus reached.

Your safe now became the great point of attack; and bravely did it resist every effort, holding secure its entire trust (property amounting to $500,000) against all the tools and ingenuity of the burglars.

The first great aim seemed to be to drill into the safe; but, although some thirty holes were made in the outer casing, the hardened iron forming the center lining turned the point of every tool. Disappointed here, they now attempted to dissect the safe and endeavored to force the strong framework apart. After removing one bar and partially cutting off another they gave this up; and all further operations proved unavailing. Our confidence in your safe has been reassured; and we would further add, for the benefit of the public and to your credit, that, had they even succeeded in getting through the outer casing or shell of the safe, which they did not do, three more thicknesses of metal still remained; and each of these, in our opinion, would have given them more trouble than the single one by which they were so completely foiled.

When the great resources of these burglars are considered, the opportunity to work *from Saturday night to Monday morning*, the great number of the best of tools in their possession, and the skill and ingenuity displayed, we have reason to feel proud of your safe.

We wish you to send the large safe purchased by us at your store to our new banking house in Greenwich street; and as soon as we get moved you shall have the old one as a trophy.

S. VAN DUZER,
President of the New York Exchange Bank.

DESPERATE ATTEMPT TO ROB THE KENT NATIONAL BANK, KENT, OHIO.

Failure of the Burglars—They could not drill the Spiegel Eisen.

On Saturday evening, the 3d of November, our bank was entered by burglars. The office of the bank being without an occupant, they had undisputed possession, and, I have no doubt, employed their time uninterruptedly till morning, in efforts to reach the treasure of the bank. But, thanks to the protection afforded by one of your Burglar-proof Safes, which on this occasion proved to be impregnable, they were foiled.

The outside, or fire-proof door of the safe was drilled and blown open. They then commenced on the burglar-proof, and after knocking off the dial of the lock, and knob that throws the bolts, they attempted to drive the lock off, but without success; they also used wedges and a heavy sledge, but failed in all. They left behind them a large assortment of tools, consisting of two crowbars, a heavy sledge, wooden mallet, two steel wedges, and a variety of chisels.

Having occasion to be at my office (which is connected with the bank) at about 11 o'clock A. M. on Sunday, I made the discovery of the aforesaid visitation and failure to open the burglar-proof part of the safe, although they had knocked off the dial-plate to the lock and otherwise disfigured and abused the safe, which prevented any one but a skillful operator or a practical manufacturer of safes and locks to open the safe.

The necessities of the case were plainly presented, and we lost no time in dispatching an agent to Cleveland to procure a proper person to open our safe. Calling at your agency, no suitable person was found. We then applied to another house in the safe business, who very kindly furnished us a practical manufacturer of safes, a person who understood the science and the manufacture of locks and safes to perfection.

He arrived, and, with the assistance of two of the most powerful men in the village, (quarrymen, who were famous for heavy strokes with the sledge-hammer), operations were commenced at $10\frac{1}{2}$ o'clock A. M. on Monday, and the work continued unceasingly till 8 o'clock P. M., when they became too tired to work longer, and adjourned.

The next morning at about $7\frac{1}{2}$ o'clock the work was again resumed with the same help, and at 11 A. M. success attended our efforts, and we again had the pleasure of knowing that our property was safe. Had it been placed in a less powerful safe, the tables would have been turned in favor of the robbers.

Mr. H. A. Kent, of the house of Kent & Co., of your city, has instructions to arrange with you for a new safe.

Yours truly,

MARVIN KENT,

President Kent National Bank.

KENT, OHIO, November 17, 1866.

To Messrs. Herring, Farrel & Sherman, New York.

The public are invited to call and see the above safes, which are now on exhibition at our store, 251 Broadway, New York.

These safes are manufactured only by

HERRING, FARREL & SHERMAN, 251 Broadway, New York.
FARREL, HERRING & CO., 629 Chestnut street, Philadelphia.
HERRING & CO., 40 State street, Chicago.
HERRING, FARREL & SHERMAN, 72 Camp street, New Orleans.

BURGLARS OPERATING

In the vault of the New York Exchange Bank.
(See page 127.)

LATER TESTIMONIALS.

GREAT FIRE AT MOBILE.

MOBILE, ALA., December 20, 1866.

Messrs. Herring, Farrel & Sherman, 251 Broadway, New York:

GENTLEMEN—The fire of December 3d, which destroyed our store, severely tested the Patent Champion Safe of your manufacture which we had in use. The contents were all preserved in excellent condition, although the safe was severely roasted. We take pleasure in adding this to your numerous testimonials of their previous triumphs.

Respectfully yours,
LEVY, WOOLVERTON & CO.

ANOTHER EXTENSIVE FIRE IN MOBILE—AN ENTIRE SQUARE WAS BURNED.

MOBILE, ALA., February 18, 1867.

Messrs. Herring, Farrel & Sherman, New York:

GENTLEMEN—My store was totally consumed by the great fire on Saturday night, February 9, which destroyed nearly a whole square of buildings in the center of the business portion of our city. I had one of your Patent Champion Safes in use. On Sunday I reached it and found it too hot to open. I left it in the ruins to cool until Monday, when I got it open. The money, papers, and books, with other contents, were preserved in excellent condition. The covers of the books were drawn by the steam; otherwise they have no appearance of having been through one of the largest and hottest fires that ever took place in Mobile. Every word and line is perfectly legible, and I am more than pleased with the result.

FERD. NEUMANN, *Agent.*

GREAT FIRE AT WILLOUGHBY, OHIO.

WILLOUGHBY, OHIO, January 24, 1867.

Messrs. Herring, Farrel & Sherman:

GENTLEMEN—At what price can you send me a No. 7 safe? I had one of yours, about a No. 4 I think, that just went through a thirty-six-hour fire, and all my books came out safe. Can you use the old one at some price? Please answer at once.

Yours truly,
W. H. MERRIAM.

GREAT FIRE AT WELLSVILLE.

HERRING'S SAFE AHEAD OF ALL OTHERS.

WELLSVILLE, N. Y., February 18, 1867.

Messrs. Herring, Farrel & Sherman, 251 Broadway, New York:

GENTLEMEN On the morning of the 1st of February our town met with a severe calamity: twenty-four buildings were burned to the ground. Our grocery store — a frame building three stories high — was consumed by the devouring flames. We had one of your Champion Fire-proof Safes in use, containing our books and papers and some bank bills, all of which came out unharmed. Although your safe was surrounded by very combustible liquids, a quantity of kerosene oil on the south side of it, and a considerable quantity of linseed, lubricating and whale oils on the north side of it; also nine or ten barrels of brandies and other liquors in close proximity to it, with nothing but a wood partition between these and the safe, all of which were burned around it.

Your Champion Safe owned by us was subjected to a fire three times as terrific and twice the length of time as the safe of another make, owned by York and Chamberlain, and our books came out in better condition than theirs.

Yours truly,
JUDD & CO.

We, the undersigned, fully concur in the above statement.

HOYT & LEWIS, Bankers.
W. T. BARNES, P. M.
R. & J. DOTY.
HENRY L. JONES.

THE GREAT FIRE IN VICKSBURG, DECEMBER 24, 1866.

VICKSBURG, MISS., February 8, 1867.

Messrs. Herring, Farrel & Sherman, New Orleans:

GENTLEMEN — Agreeably to promise made your agent, Mr. Green, I proceed to impart to you such information in regard to safes lately in the fire here as I could obtain. I have learned of two of your safes which came out all right, and without any damage. Safes of other makers were burned, so a repairer of safes informed me (he has them now in his shop), but he could not tell me whose patent they were. Since my return from the city I have but little time to be on the street; this must be my excuse for my meagre report.

Yours very respectfully,
SAMUEL FISCHEL,
With J. HORNTHAL & Co.

Many additional testimonials might be introduced where the Herring Safe has triumphed in furnace tests over other safes, as in New York, Philadelphia, Reading, &c.; but as the public are most interested in the actual results of accidental fires — where manufacturers can have no control, and as suspicion will always attach to pre-meditated trials; we confine the record of our Herring Safe to such evidences as must prove most conclusive and satisfactory to all who have books and valuables to protect from fire.

Plate No. 39.

Portable Fire Proof Bank Vault, with Banker's Chest.

SONG OF HERRING'S CHAMPION SAFE.

Yes! well may ye gaze on my iron sides,
   And well may ye murmur praise;
Like a victor mailed, I have safely passed
   Through the thunder and the blaze!
On the hero's brow ye may bind the palm,
   To his fame ye will sound the lyre;
Then how refuse a wreath to the power
   That has conquered the Fiend of Fire?
Ha, ha! how I laughed when the demon flames
   That had swept from roof to floor
Threw their wild, red arms around my waist,
   And howled before my door!
For the gorgeous wealth they had shriveled up
   Wherever their red feet pressed
Was nought to the wealth that they knew I held
   In the folds of my fearless breast.
The merchant gazed, in his terror white,
   When he saw them around me curled,
When at last the crackling beams and walls
   Were over me wildly hurled;
But I thrilled next morn to behold his joy—
   Ay! thrilled with an honest pride—
When he opened my door and found the deed
   And the bill safe side by side!
For the brain that evoked my being sought
   The secrets from sea and earth,
And together bound their glorious powers
   Before I could leap to birth.
Like the gems that the jealous genii guard,
   In the depths of the deep-blue sea,
Those secrets were hid from the eye of man
   Before they were joined in me!
Then well may ye gaze on my iron sides
   And well may ye murmur praise;
Like a victor mailed, I have safely passed
   Through the thunder and the blaze!
On the hero's brow ye will bind the palm,
   To his fame ye will sound the lyre;
Then how refuse a wreath to the power
   That has conquered the Fiend of Fire?

HERRING

SALESROOMS,
No. 251 Broadway,
CORNER OF MURRAY STREET,

MANUFACTORY,

Block bounded by 13th St., 14th St., Hudson St. and 9th Avenue,

NEW YORK.

Salesrooms, 629 CHESTNUT STREET,

MANUFACTORY,

Corner Fifteenth and Willow Streets,

PHILADELPHIA.

SALESROOMS, No. 40 STATE STREET,

MANUFACTORY,

Corner Fourteenth Street and Indiana Avenue,

CHICAGO.

SALESROOMS, No. 72 CAMP STREET,

NEW ORLEANS.

www.ingramcontent.com/pod-product-compliance
Lightning Source LLC
Chambersburg PA
CBHW031814220426
43662CB00007B/648